To Charles & Lori –

Happy ~~~~~ 1993,
and here is a New Year's
wish, that we "share"
a cultivated life
here in Washington
State ...

Jay & Janice
Soloff

A CULTIVATED LIFE

A
CULTIVATED
LIFE

A Year in a California Vineyard

VINTAGE 1991

JOY STERLING

Illustrated by Terry Sterling

VILLARD BOOKS · NEW YORK · 1993

Library of Congress Cataloging-in-Publication Data
Sterling, Joy.
A cultivated life : a year in a California vineyard / by Joy
Sterling ; illustrated by Terry Sterling.
p. cm.
ISBN 0-679-41989-6
1. Iron Horse Vineyards. 2. Wine and winemaking—California.
I. Sterling, Terry. II. Title.
TP557.S73 1993
641.2′2′09794—dc20   93-10035

This is dedicated to Forrest

FOREWORD

My parents bought Iron Horse in 1976, at a time when western Sonoma was considered both too cold and too off-the-beaten track to rival Napa. It was a run-down estate, with 110 acres of neglected Chardonnay and Pinot Noir vines, sixty-five miles north of San Francisco, on the wrong side of Highway 101. They linked up with a young, unproven winemaker, Forrest Tancer, who had planted Iron Horse when it was under lease-option to a large winery that subsequently ran out of money. Even in the rain, with their first view of the hills and the collapsing Victorian country house they fell in love with the estate and with Forrest's vision of what could be.

This is a book about how my parents became vintners, how Forrest became a wine maker, how I gave up my career as a television journalist and went to work at Iron Horse and married Forrest. It is a book about our lives, about establishing and running a vineyard, and about the business of wine. This is not a compendium of facts and figures, but a very personal view of how we make wine and the emotions we pour into it. It is a story about how we deal with making a subjective product. One which we love and want the whole world to love with us.

It's often said—truly, I think—that wines are a reflection of the people who make them. What makes a wine distinctive is the *"goût du terroir,"* the taste of the land, a recognizable quality that comes from the grapes, soil, and climate, but I think the taste, personality, and passion of the wine maker also has a lot to do with it. It's the ingredient X that sets a wine apart.

There are some 800 wineries in California, and for as many wineries, there are philosophies about how to grow grapes and make wine. Ours is just ours.

We grow all our own grapes at Iron Horse. Not every winery does. You can buy grapes from excellent growers, really fine farmers, like Robert Young in the Alexander Valley. But at a certain point the goals of the grower and the winemaker may become antithetical. Usually we both want the same things— quality and quantity—but nature doesn't always deal us that hand. Sometimes it's a poker game all the way to the end, when the grape grower might prefer to play it safe by harvesting right away, but the wine maker might want to take a risk with the weather in favor of more mature fruit, which might make more exciting wine. Having complete control is the ideal. Forrest calls it "growing wine," and that's his wine-making philosophy. We nurture and train our vineyards to express the distinguishing characteristics that come from our soils and climate then, when the grapes come into the winery we try not to screw it up.

This book focuses on 1991, Forrest's twenty-second vintage at Iron Horse. We kept a journal of the year, while my sister-in-law, Terry, followed the vintage with her drawings. The journal begins in April with the start of the growing season. Month by month, it traces the main threads of a vineyard's life: the weather, the farming, pressing the grapes into wine, and how the wines taste as they evolve from barrel to bottle.

Wine is an agricultural product. We are bound to the land and beholden to the weather. The land and the weather determine the quality and the size of our crop. We have to fit into nature's schedule. The vines must be pruned at a certain time to give the buds the best chance of surviving the vicissitudes of spring. Frost is a worry until June 1. During the summer, we hope for a long, steady growing season. If it is too cold, the grapes may never reach maturity, resulting in tight, gripping wines. If temperatures soar over 100 degrees, the vines just shut down for self-preservation. Rain in September could pump the grapes, filling them with water, diluting the flavors; if the vineyard does not dry out, it will cause rot. Every year is different and each year's crises are unique.

Instead of working *in* the vineyard, we are working *with* the vineyard. Sometimes, walking the vineyards at sunset, just looking at the particular shade of green of the leaves tells us what to do. What we experience and pick up through our senses in turn affects the decisions we make about the taste of our wine.

Harvest in September and October is the most demanding and exhilarating time for us. When we wake up, when we go to sleep, and whether or not we take a day off during those six to eight weeks is determined by what is happening in the vineyard and the winery. Crushing the grapes and fermenting the juice is a technical process, but there is plenty of room to play stylistically. Blending wine is wonderfully creative. Bottling is a nerve-racking mechanical ordeal. And as with perfume, our sales crunch comes at the end of the year.

My hope is that I can convey to you why we and most vintners are so passionate about our lives. I want you to have greater insight into the history of a bottle of wine: the full grape-growing cycle, the ups and downs of the weather, the technique, creativity, and mechanics of wine making, and the business of selling it. Plus the commitment involved. As you will see, each year's close is really the start of a new vintage.

I would like to acknowledge my husband and best friend Forrest Tancer, whose name was unceremoniously deleted from the byline because I couldn't figure out the pronouns; Dan Green who made this book happen; and my editors—Emily Bestler, my father Barry Sterling, and my brother Laurence Sterling. I also wish to thank my mother, Audrey Sterling, my sister-in-law and illustrator Terry Sterling, our chef Mark Malicki, my typists Catherine Russo, Elsa Pyne, and Gina Marsh; and Rob Akins, Maralee Beck, Howard and Jennifer Bulka, Robert Glazer, Jerry Kretchmer, Gene Moore, Sidney Moore, Gordon Mott, Robert and Judy Nyman, Anne Opotowski, David Ross, Martin Sinkoff, and Robert Squier, for their encouragement and inspiration. Thank you all.

CONTENTS

A LITTLE
BACKGROUND

IRON HORSE IS tucked away in western Sonoma County. You can't see it from the road and we don't put out any signs. You turn onto our road at Kozlowski's Berry Farm, then continue for about a mile and, just when you think you are lost, the view opens—360 acres of gentle rolling hills covered with vines that rise up to the winery with a castle wall of tall trees behind it. It's like coming into another world. This is the view that sold my parents on Iron Horse in 1976. No matter how many times we drive down Ross Station Road, we never tire of it. It is always changing, depending on the weather, time of day, and season.

We designed and built two huge, triangular planters on either side of the road, which are always filled with seasonal flowers. In September, hundreds of pumpkins on the vine line this little bit of the drive. Mounted on the stone planters are handwrought bronze horses—rampant horses, which are the symbol of the winery. Here is the first indication that you are at Iron Horse. Finally, across a bridge and behind the curtain of two weeping willows is the Iron Horse sign, the only one you will see, which says BY APPOINTMENT ONLY. Green Valley Creek cuts across the property—dividing the Chardonnay and the Pinot Noir. Each spring Father plants eight acres of vegetables along the creek bed. Even more impressive than the size is the Jeffersonian scope of his garden. My father does not just grow tomatoes, he grows forty-two kinds of tomatoes. He buys seeds from all over the world and plants them here. He has to pull himself out of the garden to get to the winery by 10:00 A.M. In the winter, this whole area is flooded. The creek overflows at least five or six times a year, inundating the bridge and washing out the road, but also providing a beautiful layer of silt for the spring vegetable planting.

From the bridge it is still a quarter mile to the winery. Next you will see a pair of wrought-iron gates with stone pillars, opening onto a long driveway lined on both sides with alternating palm and olive trees, which my brother in an inspired moment named Palmolive Drive. The dashes of color along the way change from season to season—daffodils and iris in the spring, daylilies, lavender, and a few scattered wild ginger plants in the summer. In December, olives hang on the trees, little black globes waiting to be harvested.

We make our own olive oil from these trees. Father tried to cure olives, but the most painful food experience in the early Iron Horse years was tasting his experiments. One batch was too soapy. One batch was too salty. One was so acid you could not eat it. Finally, we turned to olive oil, which has been very successful. We can get thirty gallons of extra-virgin oil from 120 trees, though last year, we didn't have any. The entire crop was wiped out by a rainstorm during flowering. This year we have a small crop, and Father has already admonished me that it's going to get pressed no matter how small it is—even if Forrest and I have to put the olives in the back seat of my car and drive them to the press in Modesto ourselves.

The palm trees are part of the architecture of Iron Horse, my father's design on the landscape. They give just the right amount of formality, and hark back to the turn of the century, when palms were very fashionable on gentleman farms in Sonoma County. They were a sign of permanence and gracious living. One summer we hosted a dinner party on this drive—500 people at one long table down the middle of the road, with lights in the trees and six chefs cooking on both sides on open-air grills. The table was a tenth of a mile long. Each chef prepared the full dinner and had his or her own staff for eighty-four people; though it was the same meal, each chef gave a different presentation.

The winery is at the end of the drive. It is a compound of Sonoma-style barns painted wine red with redwood trim. It houses our offices, the tanks and the barrels, the lab, the bottling lines, and a small tasting room. The big equipment, like the presses, dominates a concrete pad behind the winery. All around are wine barrels cut in half, spilling over with pansies in the spring and petunias and impatiens in the summer. From the winery you can see across the whole of Sonoma County to Mount St. Helena in Napa and to the Geysers above the Alexander Valley. On a clear day we can see white puffs from a dozen geysers going off like Indian smoke signals.

Iron Horse was named after an electric passenger train built in 1905. It was a spur of the Petaluma–Santa Rosa railroad line, which people took to get to the resorts on the Russian River. Before the Golden Gate Bridge, the only way to get there was to take a paddle wheeler from San Francisco to Petaluma and then hop on the train. After the 1906 earthquake and fire, most of the lumber to rebuild San Francisco came from this area via the same train. The last 1.8 miles of track from Ross Station, our road, to Forrestville was picked up in 1962. Our logo, the rampant horse, is from an old weather vane that our foreman found in the debris of a tiled Portuguese horse barn on the property that had burned down in 1968.

Iron Horse is unusual for the range of wines we produce. Chardonnay, Pinot Noir, Sauvignon Blanc, a blended red wine called Cabernets and sparkling wine. We use our own grapes from our two vineyards exclusively—from my family's property in Green Valley, the cool-climate vineyard just west of the Russian River and Forrest's family estate, T-T, in the Alexander Valley, where on any given day it is ten degrees warmer. This is the setting for what we do. From here on out in the book, you will see how our lives are intertwined with the natural cycle of the vines.

BUD BREAK

TO FLOWERING

APRIL

THE WEATHER HAS been gray, cold, and damp. The vines have barely budged for five weeks. The rains were almost biblical in March, thirty inches, filling up the reservoirs but cooling the soils and putting the growing season in abeyance. All of Sonoma County has been holding its breath for forty days.

The buzz around the county is that it's already an unusual year. We've become so accustomed to dry, early springs, and early harvests (Who knows why? It could be drought related) that having a "normal year" would be a surprise. We haven't had one in five years and we haven't had a really late harvest since 1981. The implication of a longer year, a later harvest, is that there is a greater risk of rain before the grapes are in. Right now, without sunshine, the vines are stalled and starting to yellow. They don't look happy.

Forrest walks the vineyards two or three hours a day, checking the growth and health of the vines. They differ from block to block. So does the condition of the soil, which will determine whether it is time to plow, mow, weed, sucker, and/or spray. He carries a magnifying glass, a loupe, so he can see microscopic insects and organisms. Forrest complains about how slowly it is going. He is at least five projects ahead of the crew. Every farmer must be like this—"To hell with the growing season. Let's get to the harvest"—wanting it all to be perfect.

Like all deciduous plants, grapevines are dormant during the winter. They look like gnarled trunks with bare, outstretched arms. The buds begin to swell in late March or early April, soft and fuzzy like the tips of pussy willows. At first they are pale pink, then they expand and immature green flower clusters emerge, as out of a cocoon. People assume they are the tiny grapes, but there is still another month to go before bloom, after which the real grapes will appear. By the end of April, in the glint of the afternoon sunlight, we can just start to pick up the green from the first leaves. Like all new plants, the leaves are tender and vulnerable.

Anything can happen. It can rain during flowering. It can stay cold and cloudy through the whole spring and summer, so the grapes will be nothing more than little green berries in October. Mites can cover the vineyard. And, of course, Forrest would blame himself; there must have been something out there he didn't notice or could have done. Then there is phomopsis and frost. Phomopsis is a fungus that thrives in our cold, damp conditions. It shows up first as scarring on the canes. Unchecked, it will spread to the leaves and, at its worst, to the flower clusters, which will fall off, leaving only a bare stem. The French catch-all term for this unhappy end is *"coulure."* We call it "shatter." It is almost impossible to control. How much we lose depends on the general resilience of the vines and on the weather.

April 9. So far this month, the temperature has barely hit sixty degrees. At night, it drops to forty. The sky is clear, the stars are bright, and by nine o'clock there is a deep chill in the air. By ten, the temperature is thirty-eight. We go to bed thinking there will be a frost. At midnight, the thermometer can hover at thirty-six, which triggers the alarms. There are thermometers all over the property so we can monitor the temperature even at the lowest points of the vineyard. The alarms go off both in our cellarman's house and in my parents' house, on Mother's side of the bed so Dad is sure to get up. He pulls on jeans over his pajamas, a parka, and an English hunting cap. This property lost a third of its crop annually before we put in the frost-protection system.

Down at the reservoir, José Luis Sotello has the engines warming up. It is just a matter of waiting. He is joined by Father; our foreman, Manuel Sotello, who is also José Luis's uncle; and Manuel's son, John Sotello, who is Forrest's assistant winemaker. They huddle around a space heater until the temperature drops to thirty-two-and-a-half degrees, then John checks the dew point and the relative humidity. If clouds or fog are not rolling in to blanket the sky, they reluctantly decide to engage the pumps and slowly build up the pressure in the lines. Because of the enormous pressures involved—as much as 150 pounds on each inch of pipe—the frost protection system has to be started slowly. Many nights, it is a close call. The engines are warmed and ready to go, but the temperature keeps bouncing up and down. The decision to run the system or not is important, because water is precious. We can't afford to waste it.

When it is fully operational, the system pumps 8,000 gallons of water a minute out of the reservoir. Four Mack truck engines drive the water through the underground pipes, up and down the hills of the vineyard, and into six-foot-tall sprinklers. The system can spray 140 acres of vineyard at one time. Running the water raises the ambient air temperature just as rain does.

Meanwhile, Manuel and José Luis drive around in their trucks, inspecting the system by flashlight, unplugging sprinklers in the middle of the night, making sure there are no breaks in the lines. If there are minor breaks, those valves are turned off and repaired in the morning. You cannot simply shut off the water at daybreak, because the temperature dips to its lowest just before sunrise and the grapes would freeze.

Dawn is quite a sight. The sunlight through the sprays of water and the wisps of fog on the ground make the whole property shimmer like a fairyland. If it has dropped into the twenties, icicles will be hanging on the vines. This is rare, but when it happens it is very beautiful. When the ambient air temperature rises to at least thirty-eight degrees, we can shut off the water.

We hope Green Valley Creek will continue to flow so that we can replenish the reservoir in case of future frost. The system was designed so that it can be run eight nights in a row. We can get anywhere from fifteen to twenty days of frost per season. Right now we are at the peak of danger from frost, which is in direct relationship to the length of the days. The danger diminishes as the days get longer. The latest we've ever had frost has been June 1.

Iron Horse is unique because of its water source. The cold climate allows us to produce our own particular style of wines, and the availability of water lets us preserve the vineyards during the frost season. Green Valley is a separate appellation, it's own legally recognized grape-growing area, but there are fewer than 1,000 acres of vineyards in the whole region—in good part limited to those vineyards either just above the frost level or with sufficient water for frost protection. Riparian water rights, which came with the deed to the property, entitle us to draw water from Green Valley Creek at the point where it crosses our land. We acquired patented water rights in 1977 to stockpile water in the reservoir, but only when the creek is flowing at five cubic feet per second. There's a yellow mark painted on the bridge showing how high the creek has to be before we can begin pumping into the reservoir. Anyone who has watched old westerns knows how water in the West was treasured and fought over. That has not changed.

Forrest had the vineyard sprayed twice this month with sulfur against mildew and a fungicide against phomopsis. We use a sprayer that's hooked up to the back of a tractor. It takes a week to cover the vineyard, and the driver starts before dawn, when there's no wind. The first time, $500 worth of spray was washed off because we had to frost-protect. The second time, we mixed some hot sauce into the spray—salsa, which is sold as deer repellent for $28 a quart—but it was washed off by a light rain and the deer had a feast. The succulent baby green shoots that they love will be difficult to retrain. We sprayed again at the end of the month. Forrest wasn't sure if it helped—against either phomopsis or the deer—but it made him feel better to be doing something.

Father is champing at the bit to plant the garden. It is still too cold, so he will have to content himself with starting seed trays in the greenhouse. We are tiring of frozen tomato sauce from last year's harvest. Early spring asparagus and artichokes have whetted our appetites for fresh vegetables. In a week, we will be harvesting 100 asparagus spears a day, racing to cut them before the stalks begin to turn ferny. Eaten raw, in the field they taste as sweet as baby green peas. After six weeks we will stop picking and allow them to flower out and create new tubers for the fall. The artichokes just grow. We will have 2,000 a week in May and June. To try to put a dent in them, Forrest and I steam a dozen at a time and just eat them cold over a few days, or we cut out the hearts for a salad to accompany cold prawns or baby Bay shrimp and a glass of our Fumé Blanc. At my parent's house, our chef, Mark, creates more elaborate dishes, such as lobster in artichoke broth. He says the artichokes bring out the sweetness in the lobster. They also make exotic dried flower arrangements when the fuzzy part in the center of the choke grows straight out of the heart, bright purple. All you have to do is cut them with long stalks and put them in a vase without water—they hold up for weeks. Fava beans are another story. It seems as though one metric ton ripens at once, and there are only so many ways you can prepare them.

The first of the wildflowers are in bloom, baby blue-eyes and buttercups covering two-and-a-half acres around our house. The grass is very green and up six or seven inches, so the flowers are barely visible. They are tiny things, heartbreakingly sweet, and grow very close to the ground. When we first planted the wildflowers in front of the house, our idea was to let the land return to its natural state. We had beautiful California poppies but we wanted more diversity, so each fall for the last four years we've been lightly plowing the fields around our house and planting millions of seeds. Changing the mix.

Wildflower seeds are surprisingly hard to find in bulk. They cost a fortune—$100 a pound, which covers only about a quarter of an acre—and because they are so small and light, they must be hand sown. One never knows what will come up from one year to the next. Part of their beauty is that they are very low maintenance and do not require huge amounts of water. To lie among flowers and watch the hawks glide overhead is like something out of a dream, and the place where they grow is our favorite outdoor room and picnic spot. But even walking through the wildflowers leaves an imprint, so we try to resist, at least until the red clover comes up in May.

Seeds from the wildflowers have blown into the vineyard, and begun to spread across the whole property. Forrest is helping them propagate—adding red clover and poppies to the orchard grass he is planting down the middle of the vineyard rows for a permanent turf. We disk most of the vineyard. Disking is the same as plowing, turning under the weeds and grasses to give the vineyard a manicured look and help preserve moisture. But, over time, disking causes more problems than it corrects, eventually creating a hardpan eight to ten inches deep that can seal off the ground as tightly as concrete. We are slowly switching over to a more natural way of hiding the weeds by planting six-inch-tall grass dotted with wildflowers that will make the vineyard cooler in the summer and provide a habitat for ladybugs and other insects that will help to control mites and thrips. The grass will also prevent erosion and provide a steady conduit for water to penetrate the soil. When it is mowed—about every other month—the grass will add humus to the ground, improving the quality of the soil and eventually nurturing the vines. Forrest is thinking of getting a few sheep to graze it down in the summer at T-T. But first he has to fence out the coyotes.

On April 15, we began planting the rootstock for a new vineyard above the winery on Thomas Road, which we co-own with Laurent-Perrier, the largest family-held champagne house left in

France. We coveted that property for years. It was a declining apple orchard with no water source, with the same long, cool growing season as Iron Horse, but as it adjoins our property, we can get our water up to it. Forrest says it is going to be the greatest sparkling-wine vineyard in California.

It takes a special partner to be involved in such a long-range project. In the best of all possible worlds, we will have our first crop in 1995. For sparkling wine, with four-plus years aging *"en tirage,"* that is, on the yeast, that means having our first release in the fall of 1999. Laurent-Perrier is dominated by one man—Bernard de Nonancourt, who took over his mother's company after World War II. Bernard and my father became friends the moment they met. Bernard is what my father calls a *grand seigneur.* You can tell by the way he dresses, the discreet ribbon in his lapel that shows he was a war hero, by the way he carries himself, by how perfectly he kisses ladies' hands, by his wonderful dogs, his extraordinary aim while hunting, and his absolutely amazing ability to charm and flatter. Somehow Bernard de Nonancourt compliments you in such a way that you can't help but believe every word he's saying. Father has invited Bernard and his wife, Claude, to come visit us in late October, after their harvest. My parents will visit them in December.

In the spring, rootstock looks like sticks about a foot high and an inch in diameter, with roots about two-and-a-half inches long. They are the understock, the root of the plant, which is propagated from a cutting in a nursery and certified to be resistant to a variety of diseases, most particularly phylloxera, the root louse that destroyed the vineyards in Europe and the U.S. in the late 1800s and is now beginning to reinfest California. Grape-

vines planted on their own roots have no resistance to phylloxera.

Rootstock comes bundled in bunches of fifty. The sticks are
started in hothouses and then transplanted outdoors in the
spring. In January or February, when the vines are completely
dormant, a plow is run through the field that digs the vines out
of the ground. They're loosely sorted, bundled, and put into
cold storage in wooden bins covered with sawdust to preserve
moisture. In April, they are brought to the vineyard for planting,
first being given a few days to warm up to the outside air
temperature. The big-caliber sticks will grow more vigorously.
We pay a premium for "jumbos" as thick as your thumb. We
trim and unball the roots, so that when put in the ground they
will spread out and be able to get water and nutrients from a
larger area.

Forrest deploys the crews from spot to spot on the new
property, planting where the soil conditions are right. They
don't just start at one end and work straight across. The crews
hopscotch around to where the soil is warm enough—from
fifty-five to sixty degrees—and moist enough for the roots to
grow but not so wet that the root hairs drown. It's a matter of
feel.

In one sense, planting a vineyard is strictly logistical. The
drainage is engineered. The vineyard is laid out and staked, drip
irrigation is installed, and the soil is ameliorated with nutrients.
A hole is dug at every stake, a vine planted and then covered
with a mound of dirt for warmth. The understock develops a
strong root system and at the same time the wild vine flourishes
above ground. In September, or the next spring, depending on
the weather, we will cut back the vines to ground level and graft
on the specific grapes we want to grow—in this case, Chardon-

nay and Pinot Noir for our joint-venture sparkling wine. Then we dream about what is going to grow. It will be a month before the green tendrils push out of the ground. It will be two years before they grow up the stake, four years before a crop. Ten years until the vines are really established and yield mature fruit. A vine should live for thirty years. Forrest says he has a sense of what the wines off this property will taste like. It is a special private thought that he can't describe, yet it gives him the heart to wait and to make sure the vines grow properly.

My husband became a grape grower because he loves being outdoors. He loves the growing cycle. His parents bought 460 acres in Alexander Valley in 1950 on which to build their county home, seventy miles north of San Francisco. It is a gorgeous piece of land in the northeast foothills of the Valley, on a bench that rises 500 feet off the valley floor. Forrest spent his happiest times there while he was growing up, wandering through fields of lupine, becoming passionately attached to the land. You can see it in the way he lights up when we go to T-T. In the late 1960s, when Forrest was at U.C. Berkeley, there was newfound excitement about creating really great California wines. The wine boom hit, and people were planting vineyards all over Napa and Sonoma. Forrest's father got talked into planting a vineyard even though he detested farming. His idea of being a vintner was driving a Ferrari through the vineyards, with the Sunmaid Raisin Girl waiting to greet him.

After Berkeley and a stint in the Peace Corps with his first wife, Kate, Forrest went to work for Rodney Strong at Windsor Vineyards. He did not go to enology school at U.C. Davis, but learned wine making literally from the ground up. At the same

time, my husband leased the vineyard in the Alexander Valley from his parents, with the option of leasing more land on the property for further development. They formed a company called T-T, pronounced "tee-bar-tee," like a cattle brand, for Tancer and Tancer.

Forrest bought a Massey-Ferguson 135 tractor, a rototiller, and a mower, and went out and farmed the first seven acres of Cabernet. It did not take him very long. He disked it twice, mowed it once, borrowed a sulfur machine from Bob Young down the road, hired ten men to pick grapes, and then sold the grapes to Tom Dehlinger. Today, T-T has fifty-two acres of vineyard—Cabernet Sauvignon, Cabernet Franc, Sauvignon Blanc, Sangiovese, and Viognier planted just last year, as well as one acre of Merlot, which Forrest is doubtful about because he thinks Merlot would do better in a cooler climate.

The most extraordinary thing about T-T is how much of it is left in it's natural state. Only 52 of the 460 acres are planted to vines. As the land ascends, it becomes too steep for tractors and the soils are too meager—practically adobe. Most of the land is covered with live oaks, madronas, and boulders. It would run against everything Forrest believes in to pull out 400-year-old trees or resculpt the land to make it suitable for grapes. Even the wild grasses have grown back because Forrest doesn't have animals grazing there any more. One of his favorite areas on his ranch is about halfway up, looking west across the valley with the hills still rising behind us, the Alexander Valley spilling out at our feet. The oaks are dripping with Spanish moss, and there are plenty of small streams, perfect for chilling a bottle of wine. The lusciousness lasts from February through April when there's run off, the lupine is in bloom and the moss is as thick and soft as plush. In August, this spot is dry hay with stickers. The temperature can get up to 110 degrees, so the time to come is early in the morning or late in the evening, when the wind picks up from the ocean and rustles through the trees. We can only grow grapes here that can take the heat.

This is Forrest's twenty-second vintage. He seems to me more a farmer than ever. He sold his 1990 BMW for a Toyota Land Cruiser, having decided that the BMW was a lousy ranch vehicle—he couldn't go into the vineyards with it and he couldn't keep it clean. The Land Cruiser looks very cool when it's dirty. It's a heavy-duty, four-wheel drive. It's supposed to have some mud under the flaps. Of course, Forrest is first on the block to have one, and it's fully loaded. It has a sun roof, a moon roof, CD player, and speakers in every door. Everyone in Healdsburg and Sebastopol admires it, as do all the people from New York and Beverly Hills who come to visit. The highlight of their trip seems to be tooling around the vineyards with Forrest and me, listening to Elvin Bishop on CD. All they ever said about the BMW was "nice color."

The winery looks deserted, but inside we are very busy. Each barrel is being checked and topped off, replenishing the wine that has evaporated. We are tasting 1990 Chardonnay, anticipating a June bottling. In February the wines seemed very lean. Now, they seem richer, mellower, and more complete. There is still the tang of youthfulness, but the Chardonnays have been in barrels, in contact with the lees, the yeast sediment from fermentation, for six months. Leaving the wine *"sur lie,"* or on the lees, is a time-honored Burgundian technique that makes wines rounder and richer to taste. It's a stylistic step that tones down the fruit in the wine, giving a different bouquet, a more complex combination of fruit—apple, citrus, and pineapple, subtly muted by yeast smells, oak, and the oxidation that takes place while it is in barrel. Keeping the wine in barrels allows it to age and evolve, while locking it up in a stainless steel tank keeps it the same as it was the day it finished fermenting.

Our 1988 Blanc de Noirs Wedding Cuvée, which will be released May 1, is now being disgorged. We are test-riddling, shaking and turning each bottle and doing dosage trials on our 1986 Late-Disgorged Brut and our 1988 Brut Rosé, which we hope to release in October. Riddling, disgorging, and adding the dosage, the sweetener, are the finishing steps in making sparkling wine.

You can think about making wine in huge vats or in sixty-gallon French oak barrels. Part of the luxury of *"méthode champenoise"* sparkling wine is that each 750-ml bottle is its own fermenter.

The process starts with a low alcohol, very delicate, base wine. Our Wedding Cuvée is 100 percent Pinot Noir. Our Late-Disgorged Brut is a blend of 40 percent Chardonnay and 60 percent Pinot Noir. We put the base wines in a champagne bottle, and add sugar and yeast to induce a controlled secondary fermentation. It takes about six weeks to get bubbles and raise the alcohol by a degree or so. Then the yeast cells, which have been feeding on the nutrients in the wine, stirring it up, become sated, saturated, and they die off, leaving a sediment which looks like fine sand in the bottle.

In France, the law says that in order to have "legal" bubbles, the wine must be left *en tirage* for at least a year and a day to qualify as non-vintage champagne. Vintage champagne must be aged three years *en tirage*. A tête de cuvée, which is the highest caliber, four to six years.

The longer the sparkling is left on the yeast, no matter where it is made in the world, the greater the three most important elements that define quality: bouquet, texture, and finish. When you pop the cork it should smell like freshly risen bread, which makes sense because of the yeast in the bottle. More miraculous is the creaminess and richness of texture that comes from the carbon dioxide dissolving into the wine. Thirdly, there should be a perception of sweetness in the finish, a characteristic of aging, an additional fillip that gives the wine a lift beyond just the effervescence.

Removing the spent yeast cells is a two-step process: riddling followed by disgorging. *Riddling* means turning the bottle manually or mechanically to move the sediment down into the neck, which is then put upside down in a brine solution for about fifteen minutes to freeze the neck, trapping the sediment in a small ice cube. The crown cap on the bottle is pried off and the built-up pressure shoots out the slush, leaving a perfectly disgorged, *i.e.,* clear of sediment, bottle of sparkling. The bottle is topped off—about three percent is lost during disgorging—and we add the *"liqueur de dosage"*—the ingredient X that regulates the degree of sweetness in the sparkling and puts our signature on it. We like our sparklings very dry, at the low end of Brut, .7 percent residual sugar, almost half the residual sugar of most French champagnes. It takes at least a month for the newly added dosage to marry with the wine.

We try different riddling programs, both mechanical and manual, so we can pick the best one. No two vintages respond exactly the same way. Some will riddle in a week; others require a slow, methodical program that can take months. Hand riddling has all but disappeared. The old *remueurs* of champagne may be a dying breed, because the mechanical riddlers do just as good a job, though there is always that certain lot that needs the human touch to get the yeast to wash in a straight line down into the neck of the bottle, as when the sediment is uneven or there's a defect on the inside of the glass that the yeast cells attach onto. Then the machines are too gentle; the bottles need to be jammed really hard. Here at Iron Horse we also resort to hand riddling when we are pushing to release extra cases for the holidays.

For the dosage trials, we riddle and disgorge twenty bottles or so with varying *liqueurs de dosage*. It's amazing how this small addition, amounting to barely one percent of the bottle's contents, can make such a difference. If we've done our job properly, the base wine is a perfectly reflective environment, like a room full of mirrors, so the effect of the dosage is multiplied in the manner of ripples on a pond.

The *liqueur de dosage* can be anything we want, with the single caveat that we use only grape-based products. It can be a simple syrup solution or include Cognac or esprit de Cognac, double-distilled brandy which is basically white lightning. More than just a sweetener, the *liqueur de dosage* is an enhancer, adding orchestration to the solo beauty of the wine. The wine itself must be flawless a cappella, but it is certainly more rounded with accompaniment. You can also play nice tricks with it. You can give a young wine a slight patina of age by using older reserve cuvées, or you can brighten up a "Late-Disgorged" by using young wines in the dosage.

Each year, we save several hundred gallons of our best cuvées, the base wines from each vintage. They are aged for a year in older oak barrels, blended in various combinations, and then made into a syrup by dissolving cane sugar in with the wine.

Over the years we have built up a selection of potential dosage material as varied as a perfumer's store of possibilities. There is no set formula, and as our sparklings have changed over the years, so have our requirements for the dosage. Aging the sparklings longer means we can keep them even drier, which we view as a mark of quality, since sugar tends to be used to mask any shortcomings in the wine. We also now find that our taste favors dosage wine from the same vintage as the base wine.

This is the month for tulips. My favorite is the dark aubergine, almost black one called Queen of Sheba. Then there are the really tall, bright-red tulips that open up as wide as a fruit bowl, and parrot tulips with ruffled petals. Father has brought up at least a hundred in pots from the lath house, and set them around my parents' house. Vase after vase of Dutch iris fill the rooms. In the morning, Father cuts all the iris that are in bloom, and by afternoon, new ones have opened. A huge crystal vase of lilac perfumes the whole house. We entertain three times a week now. This will keep increasing until it peaks in September, when we entertain at least five days a week. Our chef, Mark, is prepared for any number of people for lunch. Father and I blithely invite everyone to join us—our attitude is that we're having lunch anyway, so why not have company? The whole idea in all this entertaining is to get you to taste our wines the way we do. Just watching Mother set the table is an education: she mixes her silver and china and linens so that the table is a surprise, even for us. Sometimes she uses a quilt for a tablecloth, or a tapestry or Japanese obis running down both sides of the table. The only constant is the glassware—pure, clear crystal that wine shows through. She moves like an artist, setting down one thing, stand-

ing back to take in the whole picture and make sure it's balanced. For big parties, she'll start two days ahead, letting the
table evolve—adding things, taking them off. Sometimes it
doesn't work and she starts all over again. She has certain tradi-
tions. In April, she fills her most elaborate vermeil centerpieces
with farm-fresh eggs, and in the fall she arranges crookneck
squash in a low antique lacquer box to look like a flock of birds.
With such an abundance from the gardens and the cupboards,
it's easy to overdo. She says the most important part of any meal
is the conversation—it's difficult, if not impossible, to have any
if you can't see across the table. The perspective you get when
you're setting the table is very different from the one you get
when you sit down—but move anything once you're seated,
and Mother's dismay is instantly apparent.

April 21. Late Friday afternoon, Wolfgang Puck called Forrest to
ask if he could shoot at Iron Horse for his latest cookbook. He
wanted a country setting. Of course Forrest said yes, instantly,
and called Mother to alert her that he had given away her
kitchen for a day. The shoot was scheduled for Monday morning.

Wolf arrived with a pastry chef, a sous-chef, a dishwasher, a
publicist, a photographer, the photographer's assistant, and a
stylist who had her own plates, decorations, and cut flowers.
Meanwhile, our chef, Mark, was being photographed in the
garden for a story about Sonoma County cuisine. It was pan-
demonium in the kitchen, and we all still expected to have
lunch.

Watching the stylist at work, Mother could not resist offering
the occasional tablecloth, fresh flowers from the garden, and her

opinion. In the end, she took charge of styling some of the photographs. They shot five dishes and for each one she brought out an array of props ranging from nineteenth-century china to my nieces' toys. Mark set up a buffet lunch in the garden. It's always a challenge to know what to serve a famous chef, but because Wolfgang was working on a tight schedule, and every inch of counter space, every burner and oven was in use, Mark kept it simple: prosciutto, lightly dressed greens from the garden, homemade sheep's-milk cheese and baguettes for making your own sandwiches, washed down with chilled Fumé Blanc. Our greens are the envy of every chef. Mark brings whole flats up to the back door and cuts them off with scissors. We have rocket, mâche, and spicy mustard greens. Father grows his own mesclun, his personal mix of baby greens.

By five o'clock, everyone was spent. The laughter in the kitchen had died down. We popped a bottle of sparkling wine and sat in the garden to chat before Wolf and his gang headed back to San Francisco. Wolf was then going to fly home to Los Angeles. So, for him, it was one of his typical eighteen-hour days. For us, it was chaotic and tiring, but fun. It was only after they had left that we could think about the next day.

Most of our entertaining is a mix of people from the wine world, art, business, and politics. Often that includes strangers—customers of customers, friends of friends. There is no way of knowing how it's going to go—lunch can be very long or it can fly by very quickly. Generally speaking, people who are interested in wine are very civilized. And visitors are an exciting stimulus. As much as we love Iron Horse, we need to know what's going on in the world. There are dangers in being too isolated. One is that you will develop what is called a "cellar palate." If you fall too much in love with your own wines, you become too forgiving and ultimately your quality suffers. The other hazard is that you will start to believe your own press and act as if you are the lord of the manor. It's amazing how quickly you can be chopped down to size by the vicissitudes of the weather or by having lunch with someone who doesn't like your wines.

We're one month into the growing season. It's a time of anticipation modified by fear and hope for the vintage. We seem to be off to a slow start as the weather is still quite cool. What happens now will determine the size of our crop for the year.

MAY

May is when we begin training the vines—pulling off excess shoots, leaves, and flower clusters. Sulfering against mildew continues. On a clear night, it's not uncommon to find one of us roving the vineyards anticipating frost. The vines are growing rapidly. They look like little cadets marching up and down the hills. The young leaves are vibrant green-gold. It's the showiest time in the gardens and the wild flowers are at their height.

This month we will release new vintages of our Fumé Blanc and our Wedding Cuvée. Both wines have been out of stock for four or five months. They are our first releases of the year giving us something new to talk about. The focus will now turn to Chardonnay. It will be ready to come out of barrel in June, and we'll be tasting various lots on a weekly basis.

May 6. The pace is starting to accelerate. The phone starts ringing at 7:00 A.M. First it's Victor, Forrest's foreman at T-T. Then Manuel, our foreman at Iron Horse, and finally Bob Demple, a vineyard consultant who is delivering the rootstock up on Thomas Road. Forrest speaks to Victor and Manuel in Spanish about deploying the vineyard crews. On Thomas Road, they'll finish planting the new vineyards by the middle of the month. At Iron Horse and at T-T, he has the men suckering and leaf thinning.

Suckering is pulling out the shoots growing around the base of the vine. *Thinning* is pulling leaves out by hand, to open up the vines so more sunlight and air will filter through. The excess leaves aren't productive, anyway—they divert energy away from the grapes. But knowing what to thin takes experience. It's amazing what Forrest can pull off a vine. And he checks the men's work to ensure they stay focused. It's not an easy job. Working on each vine individually, getting at the leaves in the center, takes concentration and stamina. Even one acre starts to look very big when you're standing in the middle of it.

Forrest has phylloxera at T-T. When you walk through his Sauvignon Blanc, you see a number of dying vines. On most of the vines, the new growth is twelve inches high and reaching vigorously toward the sky; then we come to one where the new shoots are short and tufted, bunched up. Next to that sick one is a vine with no green on it at all—just brown sticks pointing up. It's dying in front of our eyes. Forrest cut away at it with pruning shears, trying to find some green, some life, but it was hard and brown all the way down. It will be pulled out. It's difficult to know how to react. These vines are twenty years old and have just reached their prime. It's a tragedy to yank them, but there is absolutely nothing else we can do.

There is no known antidote for phylloxera. It's an aphidlike parasite that kills the vine with its saliva while it eats away at the roots. It's a slow death. The lice colonize the roots, sap their strength, and disrupt the uptake of water and nutrients. At first, production declines. In fact, in the early stages you can get the most intense fruit—a sad irony because the next phase is a crop of flavorless "water-berries." The vine itself dies in three to five years.

Once you have an infestation, phylloxera radiates out in a circle at an ever-expanding rate. Almost every vineyard in Napa and Sonoma is susceptible. Tens of thousands of acres are at risk. And when we talk about it, many growers just shrug their shoulders and say "Join the club!" All we can do is pull out the vines, fumigate, replant on new rootstock that's phylloxera-resistant, and hope there won't be another strain.

You can't detect phylloxera when the vines are dormant. Forrest questioned the health of the vines when we were pruning. Little shoots don't give you much to work with, and he discussed what could be wrong. Maybe it was nutritional, maybe the vineyard needed phosphorus or potash, or maybe the soil was compacted or we were overcropping. In January, February, March, and April, he was still hoping that it was something else affecting the vines, something he could fix. The spring makes the vineyard look great—there's new growth. The vines have been trying, but they just aren't strong enough and after expending so much energy, they simply crash. Now, in May, the symptoms are unmistakable. Phylloxera destroyed most of the vineyards around the world in the 1860s and 1870s. They were replanted on American-grown vines. Then, in the 1960s, re-

searchers at the University of California at Davis developed a
new rootstock that was thought to be resistant as well as more
productive. Most of the premium vineyards in California are on
this rootstock, which is called AXR1. The dream in California
was always to produce quality and quantity, but the way some
growers talk you'd think phylloxera was retribution for greed.
The French meantime developed a different rootstock called
SO4. That's what Forrest is planting in the new vineyard on
Thomas Road, along with 5BB and 5C, hybrids developed for
cool, wet climates. The literature indicates that they should be
effective, especially in our soil types. No one knows if they will
be resistant to future strains. It appears that over a relatively short
period of time phylloxera adapts and mutates.

We do not have phylloxera at Iron Horse. We think it is
because of our sandy soils and because most of the original
vineyard is planted to a rather unfashionable rootstock called St.
George. When my parents bought Iron Horse, they were unhappy about having that kind of rootstock because it is a terribly
low producer, but now they're relieved because it seems to be
resistant. Also, Iron Horse is isolated. T-T is in the Alexander
Valley, where the vineyards are planted cheek by jowl. If there's
a problem in one vineyard, it will quickly spread to the next.
Phylloxera can be borne on any equipment that is used in
infested areas—on trucks, theoretically, and even on the bottom
of shoes. During harvest, we will take the precaution of having
all equipment steam cleaned if it has been used in the Alexander
Valley before bringing it to Iron Horse. Forrest has already
pulled out two acres this year. He expects to pull out another
five acres after harvest. Thereafter, we'll see. The phylloxera
seems to be marching from the base of his property up the hill.
Replanting costs $10,000 to $15,000 an acre. If we're lucky,

we'll get a crop by year four. The affected vines are intermixed with all the rest, making it very difficult to farm. You need a logical break, a whole block, so you can give the proper care to replanting, irrigating, and cultivating. Interplanting is the hardest. You end up spending more money and inevitably some of the new vines get overlooked, die, and need to be replaced yet again. One consolation is that when Forrest replants he can try new clones and trellising systems.

It's time to take last year's Chardonnay out of barrels. Forrest feels the wine is peaking. Once Forrest makes that call, he wants it out of the barrels right then and there. Any delay frustrates him. He always thinks "My God, I over-oaked it!" Does a week matter? Probably not. When to take wine out of barrels has to do with the winemaker's rhythm.

John Sotello, the assistant winemaker, will move the barrels lot by lot starting with Lot 1*F* (free run) and 1*P* (press run), 2*F* and 2*P,* and so on. The numbers represent a particular section of the vineyard picked on a particular day. Each is farmed individually, harvested separately, and the juice is split into free run—the first hundred gallons a ton that flows out of the press—and press lots—the next forty gallons a ton. Each lot is vinified separately and aged separately until we are ready to make the master blend. John knows how many barrels we have of each lot. He'll size a tank as close as possible to fit that number of barrels, sterilize the tank, sterilize the hoses and pumps. Each barrel has to be tasted to make sure it's okay. He visually inspects them to make sure there's no film, and then pumps the wine from the barrels into the tanks. He'll do one lot, wash those barrels, and then start the whole procedure for the next lot. It's very important to clean the barrels, because they are going to sit idle the whole summer. Some are always discarded because they don't smell right or they have now reached the end of their life. We hope to get five or six years of use out of our barrels.

During its time in barrel, the wine has changed both in taste and in chemistry. Small adjustments have to be made once it's in tanks. For example, we add sulfur dioxide as an anti-oxidant. We also check the heat stability, a test that measures at what temperature the wine will become hazy from unstable proteins precipitating out of it. Although this has no affect on the flavor or the way in which it ages, it is unsightly and can be easily prevented by the addition of a small amount of a fining material called bentonite—a natural inert clay from Wyoming that is the base of most natural cosmetics. The bentonite acts like a magnet, attracting the unstable proteins that then settle to the bottom of the tank and are later filtered away. Done properly, it shouldn't take anything out of the wine except the proteins. The wine will be bottled in July, after we came up with the master blend.

Father, Forrest, John, my brother Laurence, and I tasted the ten lots, which represent different sections of the vineyard and also different winemaking techniques—all the possible components of the blend. After the tasting, Father brought a sample of the best lot up to the house for Mother to taste. We met in the lab at 10:00 A.M.—the best time to taste, when our palates are awake. We tasted blind—*i.e.,* without looking at the lab labels on the bottles. Before us were set ten glasses, which we numbered, and the wines were poured out accordingly. Everyone helped pour, which made for a little bit of confusion: "Who has wine number two? Did I just pour this into the wrong glass?"

1990 CHARDONNAYS TASTING NOTES

Lot #5F: Free-run juice—honied on the nose. Broad, sweet entry. A little harsh from being so young. Long finish, a little cloying. A little hot? *Hot means high alcohol. It's perceived on the tip of the tongue.*

Lot #5P: The press lot of tank 5. Sweeter on the nose, medium entry. Interesting flavor in the mid-palate. Drops off. Short in the finish. Press fractions can be so different. *Free-run juice is more intense, livelier, zesty. Press fractions are softer, "sweeter."*

Lot #4F: Free run. Smells like spiced apples. Almost peppery on the palate. Very stimulating. A little harsh. Also, high alcohol?

Lot #4P: Sweet and floral, pressy (?) on the nose, syrupy.

Lot #3F: Butterscotch from a touch of acid—aldehyde, very grapefruity, mouthwateringly tart.

Lot #3P: Very pleasant. Nice drinking wine. It will be interesting to see if it blends in with the rest of the lots, or if we should bottle it separately as a Tin Pony. *Tin Pony is our second label, which we use for any lots of wine that for whatever reason don't rate the master blend.*

Lot #2F: Typical Burgundian nose, subtle combination of toast and lemon zest. Sweetness on the palate. The sweetness could be from the weight of the wine. *Sweetness and viscosity are sometimes confusing; so are sweetness and alcohol.* It finishes on an up note. This is a wine that can stand by itself.

Lot #1F: Sweet, spicy, and zesty. A wild and exciting wine. Like peaches and peppers. You really notice it in your mouth. It grabs your attention. *We are talking about bottling this as a reserve wine. Berry Bros. & Rudd, the oldest wine merchants in the world, have already expressed interest in buying fifty cases, which they would lay down in their London cellars and won't release for five years.*

Experiments with different strains of yeast.

There are hundred of strains of natural yeast that have been isolated from all of the world's wine-growing regions. Each is supposed to have a different flavor characteristic or a different tolerance to temperature, alcohol, etc. In most cases these experiments are akin to counting how many angels can dance on the head of a pin. However, there is always the possibility of something positive, so we try a few new strains each year.

3F with the Epernay strain: It seems mellower and sweeter. More approachable but with less zing.

3F with the Chanson strain: So fruity—pineappley and very aggressive. *Used on the East Coast with hybrid grapes. The idea of it is to bring a lot of fruit forward in the wine.* Almost obnoxious.

Tasting this way, lot by lot, the differences are so marked you can't help but think about bottling each one separately, but it's not practical and blending will yield a distinct wine we've not even conceived of yet. Experience teaches us that the sum of three great lots does not necessarily yield the best wine. At the next tastings, we will try every conceivable combination to find our master blend.

It's mid-May. The questions on everyone's mind are "When will we harvest? Are we behind, or do we need to slow down?" It's possible to peak too early and break the rhythm. Forrest now figures it will be mid-June before we have full bloom—three weeks later than normal, meaning we will not start harvest until mid-September.

. . .

May is my father's favorite month in the garden. It begins with lilies of the valley, which Father grows for May Day and Mother's birthday, May 5. It's a tradition we adopted in France, where they believe the flower brings good luck. Though Father leaves nothing to chance. He forces four sets of pots at staggered times so he's sure we will have them on the appointed days. If we are lucky, we can have blossoming fruit trees, wisteria, the first bloom of the roses, and a hill of camellias, rhododendron, and azaleas taking off all at once—ten acres of sweet smells and lustrous colors from one end of the garden to the other.

The beauty of Father's garden is that it is always changing and is full of surprises. You can't see the whole layout from any one spot—it's like a series of outdoor rooms, each with its own look and feel. You can wander for hours along twisting little paths, not knowing what's going to be in bloom around the next bend: green calla lilies, which Father propagates from seeds, or a waterfall of jasmine hanging from a twenty-foot-high branch of an old cypress. Father has been working on this garden for fifteen years.

He is currently designing and building a nineteenth-century-style grotto in the place where the original redwood water tank for the house used to stand and which is fed by a natural spring. His inspiration was the grotto at the Villa d'Este, but he became discouraged by the scale of it and downsized his project considerably. Nonetheless, our friend Rob Aiken was so impressed by the grotto that he sent Father a pink granite capital from the demolished City of Paris department store building in San Francisco to use as a garden table in the middle. One of Father's best friends, Frank Rothman, took a look at the grotto and said, "Barry, what you need here is a miracle. Someone has to take this water and be cured. Then you can forget about wine and just sell the water!" One winter's worth of moss has softened it considerably. The watermark down the middle of the back wall is becoming a rich, amber brown against the rest of the natural rocks that are a dark charcoal. This past winter, Father found an eighteenth-century stone shell that he is going to mount in the rocks, to hide one of the pipes. The stone cherub is getting nicely roughed up. Two years ago, all the employees chipped in to buy it for my parents for Christmas. It had to be pure irony, since Father is less than angelic in the office. My parents poured buttermilk on it and whey left over from Mark's cheeses to help the moss gum over it faster. Father says it will take him years to finish the grotto.

Father's rate of expansion in the garden has slowed down somewhat, but it's not too hard to figure out where he will extend his plantings next: in back of the rose garden, where he put most of the lilac—a little bit out of sight because lilac, while fantastic when in bloom, does not have the most beautiful foliage later on. This is one of the best places in the garden in April: you can pick lilac to your heart's content, as well as daffodils and three-foot-long branches of blossoms from the flowering fruit trees. The path just ends—but it's headed in the direction of where my brother and sister-in-law, Laurence and Terry, are building their home. My guess is that Father will landscape it so the grandchildren won't have to cross even a ranch road to come visit. And, of course, he wants it to be as enticing as possible.

Father has gone through various phases of gardening. In Los Angeles, his first garden was all white and very formal. In the South of France, it was various shades of red. Now, his garden is being compared to Monet's Giverny—though to my eye Giverny is still more formal than Iron Horse. The similarity lies in the jumble of color found in both gardens. Father is a collector at heart, and a catalog addict. He masses all kinds of plants and even the wildest colors seem to mix: purple pansies and bright yellow coreopsis. He is growing six different kinds of poppies as they do at Giverny, including our native California poppy, which Monet had in his garden as an exotic.

Father has over 200 different varieties of roses. Some bloom only once a year and are worth staying home to see. There are moss roses, pillar roses with six-foot-tall stems, blue and lavender roses such as Sterling Silver, Blue Girl, Angel Face, and pale-green roses with a pink rim, porcelainlike Mint Juleps—my parents' favorite, except for the name, which they hate. There are gravel paths winding in and out of the bushes so you can smell many of the blooms individually. In the center of the rose garden is a small bench under a nineteenth-century arbor covered with white climbing Honorine de Brabant and white wisteria. Sitting there is intoxicating.

Mounds of small, pale-pink climbing Cécile Brunners decorate the guest house and garden sheds. All along the edge of the vineyard when you first come onto the property are masses of peach-colored Peace roses, which are so big, healthy, and robust that except for pruning, a little dusting of sulfur, and periodic drip irrigation, they virtually take care of themselves. They only last a day or so in a vase, but you can dry the petals in a basket in the sun or in the microwave to make potpourri; and Mark distills rose essence to add to crème anglaise for desserts.

Roses and grapes are very similar. The tradition in France of planting roses at the ends of the vine rows is to point out with different colors the various grape varieties. Also, roses are susceptible to many of the same diseases as grapevines. Roses are even more sensitive, so they are an excellent bellwether for problems that might hit the vineyards.

Father's garden is mostly perennials—phlox, peonies, fox-gloves, Canterbury bells, liatris, columbines, delphiniums, hollyhocks, stokesia, astilbes, veronicas, and lilies of varying types. We know to be very careful during lily season—brush by them and your clothes get smeared with lily pollen—the brown powder from the stamens that leaves a permanent stain. To protect unsuspecting company, Father cuts off the stamens with a clipper, letting them fall into a bag so he doesn't touch them and stain his fingers. It is a costly gesture, for in three days, those blossoms will die. It still happens that new ones will open up in the afternoon and catch a guest on the pant leg. Father often shows up at the winery with orange smudges on his face and hands.

Blossoming shrubs and trees throughout the garden include blue and white wisteria, pears, cherries, dogwood, star magnolia, and tulip magnolia. Strategically placed red-leaf trees such as Japanese maples, tri-colored beech, red beech and Pieris japonicas add contrast to the forest of green. Pieris japonicas are called lily-of-the-valley trees. They're not really trees, but the blossoms look like giant lilies of the valley and have the most beautiful honeyed perfume. Weeping trees include spruce, blue spruce, weeping fir, weeping mulberry, and willows. Some are wired and weighted with rocks to induce a more eloquent sway. Potted plants for the house and the verandas are grown in two hothouses.

Father has hundreds of plastic pots containing tulips, daffodils, hyacinths, and amaryllis, which are then placed inside terra-cotta pots for display in clusters on the Victorian porches or along walks and in antique cachepots inside the house. In summer, petunias hang in baskets around the veranda. If left in place they become leggy, so there are doubles to allow rotation and trimming. The walkways are lined with crocus, grape hyacinth, and anemones in the spring. The grape hyacinth look like Wedgwood-blue grape clusters standing straight up. For cutting flowers, Father had built stone-walled raised beds of Dutch iris, chrysanthemum, gladioli, ranunculae, sweet William, Oriental poppies, and zinnias. A glasshouse also provides cymbidia and phalaenopses for winter. Late winter-blooming flowers are planted where they are easily seen from inside the house.

Father has three full-time gardeners helping him. He puts in a good thirty hours a week himself, which, as Mother says, is either worth everything or nothing. Every morning and evening the two of them walk through the garden holding hands, to see what is in bloom.

My parents met forty some years ago at Stanford University. They fell in love on their second date. Father passed the bar exam before graduation. They were married in 1952, two months out of law school, and the week of the wedding moved to Washington, D.C., courtesy of the U.S. Army. They were twenty-one and twenty-two.

In the 1960s we lived in Los Angeles, Father's hometown. Father had his own law firm and was very active in Democratic politics and civil rights. Mother accepted an appointment by then governor, Pat Brown, to serve as a California Fair Employment Practices Commissioner. As the wife of a successful young attorney and the mother of two small children, it was the first time she had worked outside the home and the first time she felt what she said really mattered. She describes it as the most challenging and frustrating time of her life. I once heard her speak at a conference in Montana. Father and I stood at the back of the room. She was very impressive. A lady came up to her afterward and said "You're so beautiful, I didn't listen to a word you said."

In 1966, when Ronald Reagan was elected governor, we moved to France, where Father practiced law and stayed out of politics.

Mother went to the School of the Louvre. My parents collected art and antiques and became passionate about French cuisine, entertaining, and culture. Mother's table became famed in Paris. She was toasted as the perfect "Parisian hostess—but, naturally, an American." Their *Belle Epoque* dining room could seat forty at dinner and had trompe-l'oeil clouds on the ceiling. Father's preferred menu included game birds *en plumage* and *île flottante*—islands of meringue floating in chocolate sauce and served in matching silver Buccellati bowls, proudly carried by butlers down both sides of the table. His favorite dinner partners were a pretend-duchess who had started out as a painter's model in the 1920s, the quite elegant, highly intelligent wife of a bourgeois banker and the beautiful fifth wife of a deposed dictator. My parents gave a dinner party for Israeli Admiral Mordecchai "Moka" Limon, who sat on Mother's right all through dinner, pleasantly chatting away while five of his gunboats were sneaking out of Cherbourg, one of the most tightly guarded harbors in France. The next morning, a correspondent for the now-defunct *Look* magazine called up and complained. "I was right there—why didn't you tell me?" But Mother could only say, "I didn't tell you because I didn't know."

At Thanksgiving an invitation was automatically extended to all visiting Americans. As expatriates, we took to heart Art Buchwald's column in *The International Herald Tribune*, in which he asserted that Thanksgiving is the one day of the year when Americans eat better than the French. But try explaining that to a chef who had never even heard of sweet potatoes. *"Avec marshmallows? Quelle horreur."*

Mother learned the hard way about how strict the French are about vegetables. After one dinner party, one of her guests said, "Audrey *chérie,* I'm only telling you this as a friend, but one never serves tomatoes at a formal dinner." Apparently, certain vegetables are peasant food. Another mistake she made was going into the kitchen on the chef's day off. She had every pot and pan scoured, causing the chef to throw a fit and threaten to quit because she had destroyed the months of work he had put into massaging exactly the right amount of oil and seasoning into the pans.

Father loved the Paris apartment. It was a big white elephant on avenue Foch, with marble floors and crystal chandeliers. It made him feel as if he had gone back a hundred years and was living the life of a nineteenth-century French gentleman. The apartment came with three *caves*—several floors underground— each of which could hold 5,000 bottles. The thought that to live up to his nineteenth-century image would require 15,000 bottles of wine discouraged even Father. He sealed off two of the *caves* and he and Mother proceeded to travel through France's wine-growing regions. Along the way they became increasingly interested in buying a château. One night they went to a grand wine tasting in Paris at the three-star Taillevent restaurant. It was a blind tasting for professionals and connoisseurs. Nonetheless, Father was the only one who guessed the mystery wine, a Bourgeuil that he had consumed in vast quantities with Alexander Calder in Calder's studio in the Loire Valley. Father says he recognized it from the way it burned his throat. The next morning, he was written up in the *Trib* as one of those rare Americans who bested the famous French tasters.

My parents spent five years in France looking for the perfect place. Sometimes the château was right, but the wine was not.

In the Dordogne they found the ideal château—small, built for a ballet dancer who was the mistress of Louis XVI's brother—himself to eventually become king. But no matter how elegant, it could not make up for the fact that it produced a second-rate sweet wine sold mainly to the coldest regions in Scandinavia. In Bordeaux, they found what they thought was the perfect vineyard, a classified Cru Bourgeois in the Haut-Médoc. The place, however, was a ruin. The only occupied room in the château was dusty and filled with mementos. My parents were certain the stuffed dog on the couch was a deceased pet who had been immortalized by the local taxidermist. All the meetings went well, and money was deposited with the local *notaire*. Then Father discovered that the property was being "overproduced." The widow was selling a classified cru bourgeois from twenty-five hectares (approximately sixty acres) when she only had the right to produce a classified wine from 60 percent of her property. The other 40 percent would have to be sold—even though it was the same wine—as an unclassified Bordeaux, and although no one might bother a French widow, Father felt the French authorities would have no compunction in insisting that he live by the rules. They pulled out of the deal. Force of circumstances both business and personal brought them home to California, where Mother renewed the search.

This year was Mother's sixtieth birthday. We started celebrating the third week of April and petered out on Mother's Day. One of the parties was at Hog Island Oyster Farm, a funky beachfront oyster depot just south of the Sonoma line in Marin County. This was Mother's choice. It seemed strange to be entertaining away from home when the gardens were at their height, but how many weddings and birthdays can you have in one place?

And, for Mother, Hog Island represents the Northern California coast. So Father just added potted plants—including lilies of the valley—to the truckloads of party supplies that were transported from Iron Horse to the beach.

Half the fun was getting there: it took forty minutes to travel twenty miles of little winding roads. We cruised through small western towns like Occidental, Bodega, and Freestone, with their nineteenth-century wooden churches and one-room schools, through stands of tall trees—redwoods and pines, with luscious ferns underfoot, wild rhododendrons and three-foot-tall Queen Anne's lace, past dairy farms and then out to a wide expanse covered with wild iris and grazing sheep, just before dropping down to the ocean. You tend to forget that parts of California still look like this. You can't go more than twenty miles an hour—especially us that day, because Forrest and I had the birthday cake from Larkcreek Inn in the trunk of the car. At the party, we had sparkling with oysters and clams fresh out of the water, and shucked at the source. We sat on hay bales and ate lobsters steamed in a sandpit and buffalo burgers cooked on open-air grills. The wines were our 1988 Chardonnay and our 1983 Cabernet Sauvignon in magnums. What else would you serve with buffalo burgers? And Cabernet with a dark, rich devil's-food cake is one of mother's favorite food-and-wine combinations. We danced to Frank Sinatra songs and roasted marshmallows on a driftwood bonfire as the sun set on the water.

I don't know how I got to be so lucky. The only thing I can say in my defense is that at least I appreciate it. I have long since given up worrying whether I deserve it or not. I've got the ball and I'm running with it.

JUNE

June is the month for flowering. It's the end of frost season. The days are long. The hills are carpeted in green. The rows look like continuous hedges. Several major selling expeditions are scheduled this month. June is traditionally a strong month for sales, because of weddings, graduations, and a general social whirl that seems to get people drinking more wine. It's the month for summer wine festivals in Aspen, Telluride, and—every other year—in Bordeaux. It's a tricky time to leave the vineyard: we're leaf-thinning and cane-cutting, mowing and disking, and we are anxious about fruit set, so I usually travel alone.

To make wine, you have to sell wine. We have distributors in almost every state and agents abroad, but it is imperative to get out and see firsthand what's happening in the real world, what my lawyer/father calls "due diligence." That's my job for the family.

I joined the winery in 1985. Robert Mondavi was my role model. I couldn't believe his energy. All I heard was "Robert Mondavi was just here" or "Robert Mondavi is coming." It was like following the trail of where George Washington slept. Ernest Gallo was also legendary for being everywhere. At over eighty, he would still make surprise sales calls to personally ensure that his wines were floor staked front and center in every store. I quickly learned that you have to love travel and intense PR in order to succeed in this business. Not to mention eating. Sometimes it feels as if I'm just moving from one meal to the next. Other times, the schedule is so tight I feel like a politician running for office.

The wine business—and the wine merchant's search for business—goes back thousands of years, to the time when wine was transported in barrels on wickerwork boats down the Tigris and Euphrates rivers to the great cities of Ur and Babylon. This makes wine selling almost the world's oldest profession—though it has always carried an aura of respectability. A *marchand de vin* is depicted in one of the stained-glass windows in Chartres cathedral, and in the nineteenth century the English wine trade was considered a very acceptable, gentlemanly endeavor.

In one sense, wine selling is a relatively simple business. We make a product that we sell from vintage to vintage, *i.e.*, *x* numbers of cases in twelve months. It's easy to figure out how many cases I have to sell every month to be on track.

I travel primarily in the spring and the fall, because that's when we trot out new releases and restaurateurs change their menus and wine lists to match the seasons. Wine lists used to be practically carved in marble, but now they are on computer and can change with every sales pitch. June is my last chance to sell large quantities of wine before the habitual summer lull, when beer is king in the market.

Wine selling is also very competitive. The recession has made it even more so, and it certainly didn't help that *The Wine Spectator,* the most widely read wine magazine, trashed the entire 1989 vintage for California Chardonnay—which, of course, is what we're all selling this year. That was the year which quickly became known on the street as the "vintage from hell." It rained in September in 1989, resulting in diluted flavors and generally insipid wines. Some wine buyers won't even taste 1989. They say, "That's okay. I'll just wait for the 'ninety." Buyers who only want your best are called cherry pickers. Those who turn up their nose at everything are branded cork sniffers.

How I sell wine is extraordinarily straightforward and old-fashioned; it's like the way my grandfather did business. One of the pleasures of the wine trade is that it is built on personal relationships and visibility. A great review can sell thousands of cases in two weeks, but every month a dozen wines score ninety and above in *The Wine Spectator* and from Robert Parker, possibly the single most important wine critic.

I come by selling naturally. My father's father, known as J.D., was one of the all-time great salesmen. Grandpa Dave could sell air. He was a self-made man, a wildcatter, and a big spender. His idea of a great night out was to have everything prepared table side—Caesar salad, steak Dianne and cherries jubilee. His favorite restaurant in Los Angeles was Perino's, where he and my grandmother dined every Thursday night. And my own father first met some of our best customers when they were just starting out at Perino's as waiters and maître d's.

I learned from my grandfather that the most important thing about selling is to believe in your product. That way, you never give up, because if you love your product, then you never feel rejection, just sadness at a customer's blindness. You know they're going to come around and you remind yourself to be gracious about it. Passion is without doubt the most compelling sales pitch, so long as it doesn't turn to arrogance.

Selling wine in the United States is like selling to fifty different countries. With the repeal of prohibition, each state was allowed to adopt its own liquor laws. It is illegal for us to ship directly to a licensee—a store or a restaurant—let alone an individual in all but three states (California, Oregon, and Washington). UPS won't even handle wine outside of California. We have to go through a distribution company that serves as a middleman between the winery and the customers. It's a three-tier system, from production to wholesale to retail. Franchise states, like Georgia, protect the distributors. We can't change companies no matter how poorly they perform. We would have to go through a hearing with the state authorities to show cause, and failure to sell our wine would not be considered sufficient justification. It is like being unhappily married . . . for life. Control states such as Pennsylvania got into the wine business themselves. There, we sell to the Pennsylvania State Liquor Control Board. The storekeepers are civil servants. They are not allowed to make recommendations to customers. A number of states, especially in the Bible Belt, still have blue laws. Texas is dry in parts. You can cross a county line just by crossing the street, and be unable to buy a drink. The TACB (Texas Alcohol Control Board) prohibits winery owners from pouring their own products at trade tastings as an inducement to buy alcohol.

Historically, Americans have always been puritanical about alcohol. Wine is not considered the all-American drink, even though Thomas Jefferson made wine at Monticello and wine is now produced in forty states. In Europe, wine is part of everyday life. Children are raised on water and wine at the family dinner table. We still get raised eyebrows when Forrest's fourteen-year-old, Michael, helps us open bottles at tastings.

My first year with the winery, I traveled constantly. I had no idea how the business ran; I wasn't much of an authority on winemaking; I clearly didn't know how to schedule my trips. Once

I found myself in New Jersey in August, working the market with a young saleswoman from our distributorship. In New Jersey, they permit pool buying—a consortium of retailers can consolidate an order to get the maximum volume discount from the distributors. One of the biggest groups in the state is headed by a retailer in the borough of Ho-Ho-Kus, who gave me some on-the-job training. It was 110 degrees outside—maybe not literally, but it felt that way. Oppressively hot and sticky. I was wearing the most exquisite sky-blue silk shantung suit, lined in beige silk, with a navy-blue, spaghetti-strapped suede camisole, stockings and high, high heels. For reasons that must go far beyond miserliness, the owner had the air conditioning turned off in his store. His wife and sons who worked with him were sweaty. All the bottles in the store were sweaty. And this man laid into me, before I even had my first sample uncorked, about California wine pricing. "Who do you Californians think you are?" he said. "There's plenty of expensive wine in the world and it's all French." He practically spat our 1983 Chardonnay in my face. He told me it was flavorless. Well, he was right about that—1983 was a bad vintage—but by this time I was so hot that I had sweated right through my suit. I shoved the corks back into the bottles. "I guess it's just a matter of taste," I said, and stomped out, dragging the salesperson behind me.

She was sputtering, "Sir, what about our other products?" but I yanked her out the door saying, "Today, you're working with me and we're leaving." Bottom line. I regret walking out on that account to this day. First of all, it's my job to stay and argue the merits of our wine, all day and night if need be. Secondly, the sales rep had to go back in there weekly. That's how she earns her living. I certainly didn't help her relationship with this buyer, so how is she going to feel about Iron Horse against all the other wines in the distributor's portfolio? It's unlikely we'll be her first priority. Years later it's still embarrassing, since our New Jersey distributor must court this retailer for his support and buying power on behalf of our wines, confirming the basic business adage, "who needs enemies?"

Ultrapremium wines, like Iron Horse, are called "hand sells," because they require specialized knowledge and commitment to be successful. It's nothing like selling liquor. In fact, there's a certain amount of elitism to being a wine sales specialist, an elitism you just don't find in being a liquor head. A saleswoman I rode with recently said, "You can be dead and sell liquor." Liquor salesmen reputedly can only talk discount and incentives. Wine salesmen have to be motivated by more than money, prizes, and trips. Wineries our size can't afford such spiffs. We are most successful with people who have a special feeling for us and our wines. It's a cliché, but wine selling is a people business; you can't become cynical about quality being the most important factor. Most wine salespeople are college educated, and as a result, the caliber of the people working for the big distributors who handle both wine and liquor has changed from the oldtimers to very bright go-getters.

There are a few one-of-a-kinds out on the street. Like Big H in Manhattan, who sells wine, spirits, and a bottled water he imports on the side from Europe. Big H makes his sales calls in a black stretch limousine. He has two drivers to cover two shifts—day and night—so that he can hit all the different kinds of customers he handles and amortize the cost of the car. Forrest rode with him one afternoon. They mainly called on Mom-and-Pop grocery stores and Chinese restaurants. After dark, he hits the bars and higher-priced restaurants and, much later, the clubs. He also has the Wall Street territory. Down there, he walks to his accounts, while the driver takes off to pick up a check from another customer. Nothing under the table. Collections are part of sales. It is common practice among big distributors that a salesman can "go out on the hook" for an account who otherwise would be put on a C.O.D. If payment is delinquent, it comes out of the salesman's pocket.

The first tier of wine sales is to our distributors. They are our primary customers, and we sell to them at F.O.B. prices. F.O.B. means "free on board"—what our wine costs at the point of pickup. Once it's on their truck, they own the goods. To price one of our wines, Forrest, Father, and I study our costs, taste the wine together and decide on the retail price we think it should sell for. Then I call Matthew Green, our wine manager in New York, and we work backward. To arrive at F.O.B., we take off the retailer's profit, the distributor's profit, state taxes, and transportation. That sets the national price. After that, it's basic supply and demand economics. If the wines sell too quickly, or if our distributors aren't squawking, we up the ante.

Distributors come in all shapes and sizes. We are represented by some of the biggest: Peerless Importers in New York, Young's Market in California, and Glazer's in Texas, Arizona, Louisiana, and Arkansas. The three combined buy over 60 percent of our wine. We are also represented by small wine-only houses like Direct Imports in Illinois and Ruby Wine in Massachusetts. Most of our distributors tend to be family owned, including many of the big ones. Having that level of commitment from the owners is very important to us.

The distributor's job is to pick up, warehouse, sell, invoice, take the financial risk, provide additional services like printing winelists and building displays, deliver the wine and do market surveys to track sales for each supplier. At their best, big distributors pull a lot of weight in the marketplace, and, as a result, can deliver our product more efficiently and cost effectively than any other system. The challenge of a big house like Peerless is that it has eight thousand SKUs—line items—in its book. Iron Horse represents a fraction of their inventory, but requires a huge amount of their attention. As my father said, "It takes as long to make a small deal as it does a big one," and how to make it worth their while is the key. Large or small, every distributor works in a slightly different way. They are like secret societies, and have very arcane ways of functioning. John Magliocco of Peerless describes them as puzzles. He says "You have to find the key that makes each one work." Vern Underwood of Young's says that you have to keep pounding on the sales people to get results. For Robert Glazer, president of his family firm, it's knowing exactly where we want to end up at the end of the year, so they can budget themselves every two or three months. That's one reason why salesmen hate to do "ride-withs"—having a winery rep ride with a salesmen from account to account—at the end of the month. They have quotas to make.

In the absence of any great PR or marketing coups, my job is to doggedly communicate everything there is to know about Iron Horse on every level, from the owners of the distributorships, to the wine managers, to as many sales reps on the street I can capture, and to their customers—the retailers and restaurateurs, the wait staff and store clerks who will be actually recommending our wines and, if I can get to them, the ultimate consumers. I need to sell from top to bottom. I make sales calls almost every day, in different cities. Each trip includes appearances at wine tastings, where I stand behind a table, smile and flog our wines. "This is our 1989 Chardonnay. The grapes come from my family's . . ." I also occasionally do wine-maker dinners—a form of dinner theater, where I am part of the entertainment and, hopefully, attract seventy to eighty people to the hotel or restaurant; usually on a Tuesday, to generate business on a slow night. I fly in, put on a great-looking dinner suit, high heels, and jewelry, stand up from my seat at the table with a glass of wine in my hand and sing like a canary about Iron Horse. We taste six or seven of our wines, along with having an elaborate meal. It is my chance to make disciples of doctors, lawyers, and bankers in various cities. The format is usually the same and I get tired of hearing myself speak, but the people are very nice and it takes only the slightest spark of interest to get me going. My main concern about doing wine-maker dinners is the fear that nobody will show up.

Last week I did a wine-maker dinner at the Rittenhouse Hotel. It's a gorgeous hotel, newly refurbished and with an adjacent condominium development on Philadelphia's "Main Line." For them, wine-maker dinners serve two purposes. One is to please a steady group of sixty to seventy reliable customers who really enjoy multicourse tasting feasts. The second is to entertain prospective condo buyers. For me, it was a chance to get to know the hotel people; primarily, the food-and-beverage director, the dining-room manager, and the wait staff, in the hope that they will like me, love the wines, and sell them like crazy.

At 5:00 P.M. or 5:15, while they were setting up for dinner, I was given ten minutes to make a presentation to the waiters.

This brief tasting and the reaction of the guests that evening will determine whether Iron Horse will be a success in this account.

The guests arrived at 7:00 P.M. and were offered a glass of sparkling as an aperitif. Hors d'oeuvres were passed while we were waiting for everyone to show. This is when I'm most nervous. Once everyone was seated, there was only one empty table. The maître d' introduced me. He began by thanking everyone for being there. He said how pleased he was that the wine-maker series was going so nicely. "Last month," he said, "we had Sue Hua Newton (a former Chanel model with a Ph.D. in marketing), here from Newton Vineyards in Napa, and tonight we have Joy Sterling from Iron Horse, and believe you me, ladies and gentlemen, this gal has been around."

I'm not sure exactly what he meant by that, but of course he's absolutely right. I've got it worked out so I'm in Florida and other warm-weather spots in February, France in June, New York in October, and Yosemite in December. I raised my glass of sparkling wine, and offered the first toast, "Everything you have ever heard about the glamorous life of a wine-maker is absolutely true."

I worked the tables in between courses like any good hostess, answered questions and handed out my card. The chefs came out with dessert. Everyone applauded and slowly the evening wound down. Most of the guests left by eleven o'clock. I tried to stay up with the chefs, but I got sleepy. I love the chefs. They are fun-loving, primarily interested in quality, and rarely ask me about price.

There is a very suspicious parallel between where we sell wine and where I like to go. It's stimulating to be in big cities and I love staying in hotels when the service is great. The only thing that makes it seem like work is that Forrest rarely comes with me. I have even conquered time-zone changes, and can curl up into a ball in an airplane seat and sleep. I work out religiously, so that I stay enthusiastic about going to dinner. After two or three cities, it takes a mental effort for me to remember my hotel room number, but other than that I adapt easily. If anything, I get spoiled by room service and being able to just drop the towels on the floor.

It gets a little chaotic when we're all traveling. The only way to keep track of the comings and goings is with our "Month-at-a-Glance" calender of events, which we lovingly call "Life at a Glance." Moyne Martinez in our office updates it on the computer every two or three days so we can always see what's looming ahead.

MONTH AT A GLANCE
Updated June 10

WEDNESDAY, JUNE 12

FRT, United Winegrowers mtng at Simi at 8:00 A.M.

12 PM. FRT, photo shoot at Hanks Studio, 635 Byrant St. S.F., for Meals-on-Wheels benefit. Contact person, Jennifer Bulka, (415) 566–6414.

Lunch, 12 noon arrival, T.H. and chainstore merchandisers, "new trends in marketing." Party of 4. Joy to handle.

BHS & AMS, Wine Institute Week. Washington, D.C. Staying at the Willard.

6:00 P.M. Lee Baily's Wine County Country Cooking promotional event at Garden Valley Ranch, Petaluma. (707) 778–8769. Contact Carol Lee Fisher of Random House.

THURSDAY, JUNE 13

BHS & AMS, Wine Institute Week, staying at the Willard.

2:15 P.M., Tour and Tasting for Jordanian Ambassador to the U.S. Hussein Hammami and World Affairs Council of Sonoma County President, James Odom (707) 523–3227. Party of 8. Followed by sparkling wine up at the house. LGS to handle.

Forrest and Joy leave for France.

FRIDAY, JUNE 14

BHS & AMS Wine Institute Week, staying at the Willard.

Barbara Dixon, V.P. Motion Picture Association, lunch, noon arrival, Per AMS.

3:00 P.M., Mike Bergin bringing out the etched bottles for the Sonoma County Auction.

SATURDAY, JUNE 15

Stuart Gross of N.Y., party of 2. He won this luncheon. See event file.

Bonnie and Steve's wedding.

SUNDAY, JUNE 16

Chaine de Rôtisseurs Dinner at Sonoma Mission Inn. Note: this is black tie.

MONDAY, JUNE 17

Vin Expo begins.

Looking at our schedule, it's hard to imagine where vineyard work fits in. By mid-June the vines are growing two inches a day. Bloom has begun. The blossoms are the palest of yellow, and there is a subtle, sweet perfume in the air. The new shoots are beginning to bend over the wires and cascade toward the ground. It's like watching children grow. Forrest is like an anxious parent. If he leaves the property he calls in three times a day.

It takes at least three years to build a prestigious brand name. The basic strategy is to establish the label in all the top restaurants: being on the wine list of restaurants like Spago in Los Angeles and Aureole and Le Cirque in New York is the most important third-party endorsement you can win. In every market, there are a certain number of "beacon" accounts you have to be in. These are not hard to discover, and ultimately it's my job to make sure our wines are properly represented in such places. I personally make calls on 250 customers across the country. The most important thing I've learned is that you can't take any of them for granted—especially customers who are also good friends. Luckily, I thrive on the public-relations side of the business—as my other grandfather, my mother's father, always said, "Do what you love and you'll never work a day in your life."

We Californians have come to dominate the U.S. wine market in the past ten to fifteen years. Today even New York City's most diehard French restaurant carries a good range of California wines, and, more important, they sell—even when they're listed in the back of the wine book.

Many factors have led to the ascendancy of California wine, constantly improved quality and changing tastes in food among others. The way we eat today speaks to the vibrancy of California wines, and the stratospheric price of fine European wines certainly helps, along with our growing chauvinism. More and more, America is coming to see itself as a wine-producing nation.

The export picture is completely different. The French control the world market, and have done so for a century. In Japan, for example, French wines represent 49 percent of the market, California only 8 percent. Italian wines are doing much better than Californian because of the growing popularity of Italian restaurants in Japan. Californian cuisine really didn't go over there at all—or so we're told. In England, Australian wines are beating us largely on price. Nonetheless, we are making a valiant effort at establishing a toehold in the export market. We now sell in Canada, England, France, Switzerland, Sweden, Denmark, Hong Kong, Singapore, Thailand, and Malaysia. Canada is growing the fastest for us. We travel to all these markets, and this year Forrest and I participated in our third Vin Expo.

Vin Expo is the biggest wine fair in the world. It takes place every other June in Bordeaux. There, in one week, under one roof, we can see what's happening worldwide with wine on every level—production, quality, sales, pricing, technology, and packaging. Like the Book Fair in Frankfurt or the couture collections in Paris, it's essentially a trade show, albeit a very fancy one. Every serious wine producer in the world is there, vying for the attention of fifty thousand wine buyers and 800 journalists. Everything is available for tasting, and the samples are poured by the owners and wine makers themselves. It makes us realize that we're just a drop in the bucket.

You have to walk through Vin Expo to believe it. The exhibition hall is one kilometer (0.6 miles) long. There are over 2,000 wines and spirits from ninety countries: first-growth Bordeaux, $90-a-bottle Burgundies, tête de cuvée champagnes, expensive Italian wines, very exciting wines from New Zealand, the best inexpensive wines from Chile, even less-expensive wines from Bulgaria, vodkas, Polish cherry brandies, single-malt Scotches, Cognacs and Armagnacs, eaux-de-vie. Without moving more than five feet, you can taste wine from Alsace, Australia, or Spain. Ten thousand tasters a day from all over the world are jammed into the hall. The attendees are buyers for big distributors, some representing entire countries, airlines, cruise-ship lines, major restaurateurs, and the international wine press. Some of the booths are very elaborate. The Schlumberger booth looks like an Alsatian Disneyland, complete with oompah-pah band. Bollinger's booth is a formal nineteenth-century drawing room. The California Pavilion is conservative by comparison.

We exhibit as part of an ad-hoc group of California wineries founded by the Robert Mondavi Winery in 1987. This year the California Pavilion is made up of thirty wineries. The California

Wine Institute has taken over the administrative chores—applying to the federal government and the State of California for export funds, for instance. All costs are shared equitably. It may take fourteen months to get reimbursed by the U.S. government, but, bottom line, it will cost $12,000 for Forrest and me to participate. That's the minimum we can get away with.

We flew to Paris to "adjust" for two days. One night we dined at Tan Dinh—a great Vietnamese restaurant on the Left Bank, famous for its wine list. They have a number of California wines, so it was no surprise that we ran into a bunch of our confrères. On the train to Bordeaux the next day, it felt as if we knew everyone on board. We hardly ever see other winery people at home, only at promotional events or crisscrossing each other in the marketplace, and now thirty of us were going to be together for five days in a 700-square-meter booth (roughly 7,000 square feet).

The Pavilion was designed to look like a rambling California ranch-style house made of wood, and the space and the construction cost $250,000. Each winery has its own little booth inside the Pavilion. We wanted the Pavilion to be open, airy, and inviting—drop-ins at this sort of event can be very important—so there are very few partitions. The minimum size we could "buy" was twenty-four square meters (roughly 240 square feet)—though two wineries could share it. We are sharing with Chalone this year. There isn't much privacy. Quite often we will have a group of buyers at our table, while Mike Richmond and Larry Brooks from Chalone have another bunch at theirs. They even pour our wine for us if we step away. Manfred Esser of Cuvaison, possibly the most intense salesman in the industry, tried to help us get a distributor for our sparkling wines in Germany. He sent the buyer to see us three times, but much to

Manfred's disapproval we managed to miss him every time. We tried to follow up but, not surprisingly, the man bought from another winery.

We had shipped over five cases of our sparkling, two cases of Chardonnay, one case of Fumé Blanc, and two cases of Cabernets to use as samples. We figure we can get twenty tastes to a bottle. Ten cases is a relatively conservative amount, but it sets a limit. We have found that we go through however much wine we bring.

The first morning we both stayed in our booth, diligently pouring tastes until lunch. Proper etiquette is for us to taste with each visitor. We swirl the wine in the glass to release the bouquet, take just a sip and then spit it out so as not to absorb too much alcohol. By afternoon, we already started taking turns in minding the booth, going out to taste other wines, and walking around to see what everybody else was up to.

At our first Vin Expo, we were invited to tour Margaux and have dinner at Yquem. Forrest and I simply abandoned our booth to make these engagements. Château Margaux is not the kind of place where you feel you can just drop by. It's so imposing it's not hard to find, but there aren't any directional signs. Once you enter the gates, clearly you're supposed to know where to go or you wouldn't be there. We presumed we weren't supposed to knock on the front door of the château so we wandered around until a gardener directed us to an inner courtyard. We still weren't sure what to do: there was no parking lot, no reception area, certainly no tasting room. The layout of the property was very formal, with perfectly manicured gravel driveways between sections of the vineyards. We tried several of the doors around the courtyard, eventually finding one in the corner that led to the reception room—a traditional salon with a collection of framed Hermès scarves honoring the first-growth châteaux—one with their coats of arms, another with renditions of the chateaux around the border and Yquem in the middle. My favorite had just splotches of color, different shades of bordeaux around the edge—presumably a perfect match with the wines—and of course yellow-gold in the center.

In the waiting room we were surprised to see Gil Nickel, Larry McGuire, and Dirk Hampson—the owner, PR director, and winemaker from Far Niente: The five of us were taken around by the young estate director, Paul Pontallier, who showed us the entire facility, including the area where the grapes are hand sorted, an outbuilding where the coopers work (Margaux still makes some of their own barrels) and the famous barrel rooms. The first is a huge underground cellar built in the nineteenth century, with eighteen columns, vaulted ceilings, and recessed lighting. We also saw the new one which is at least ten thousand square feet and as beautiful as the nave of a cathedral.

After the tour, Paul escorted us into a brightly lit, wood-paneled lab, where we tasted barrel samples of the 1986 vintage—an excellent year—which we spat into stainless-steel sinks. The owner, Corinne Mentzelopoulous, poked her head in. She is a blonde about my age, who inherited Margaux from her father, a Greek chain-store tycoon. She was leading another group of people around and trying to discreetly coordinate with Paul so the two tours wouldn't collide. "See," I whispered to Forrest, "they have to give tours, too."

At Château d'Yquem, Forrest and I were thrown in with a busload of international enologists—not always the most scintillating group in the world, but the evening was perfectly enchanting. At sunset, we sipped champagne on the stone terrace overlooking the vineyards. They served Moët Brut Imperial, not my favorite but still one of the best-selling champagnes in the world—and it was impressive seeing it poured out of Salmanazars—9-liter bottles.

Dinner was served in the eighteenth-century ballroom, which was furnished with round tables and gold chairs. Forrest and I were seated with our host and hostess, the count and countess.

I expected to have a broad selection of Yquems with dinner—dessert wine and foie gras, for example, is a classic combination—but the Count and Countess de Lur-Saluces served the wines of their confrères and only one vintage of their own, which they held until the cheese course. At that point, the count announced that we had a choice: to stay with the red—some first growth or another—or switch to Yquem. It seemed only polite to taste the Yquem at the first opportunity. I tried to play it safe by taking a complete selection of cheese from the platter, hoping my host would give me another clue, but he stayed with the red. I later learned that Roquefort is the one cheese that goes with Sauternes, and is another classic food-and-wine combination.

After dessert, coffee was offered in the salon in demitasse cups served by the butler. I was surprised to learn that the Lur-Saluces do not live at the châteaux, but on another of their properties. Yquem is used primarily for entertaining. I asked the count about his travel schedule, and he said he came to the United States fairly frequently, primarily for collectors' dinners at which Yquem aficionados get together and taste very old vintages, some no longer available even at the château. He said the oldest family vintage he had tasted predated the American Revolution.

The Bordeaux Châteaux definitely have the home court advantage. They seem to be very cooperative in securing Bordeaux's image as the wine capital of the world and, like an oligarchy, rotate which one is going to host Vin Expo's crowning event: La Fête des Fleurs. This year the party was thrown by an estate in Graves, Château la Louvière, where the menu showed a strong California influence—probably because one of the chefs, who happens to be married to the proprietor's daughter, is now behind the stove at Chez Panisse in Berkeley. The fête began with spiny lobster tail formed into a flower in a shallow bowl of bright-red gazpacho. The second course was a wild-mushroom-infused ragout of julienned strips of duck and beef presented in a mold covered with carrot slices. The rest all sounds very French. Thick slabs of foie gras *en gelée* (reviving an ancient custom of serving foie gras as the main course), followed by a selection of cheeses from Bordeaux's master *fromager* Jean d'Alos. Dessert was mixed fruit in a citrus syrup with a crumbly Basque-style cake to soak up the juices. The meal was specifically designed to go with a battery of the most elegant wines from Graves and everything had been exquisitely planned. No expense or effort was spared on the place settings, crystal, armies of waiters and sommeliers, and tactical organization.

The rest of us poor visiting exhibitors were expected to entertain in restaurants or rented châteaux, though we Californians surprised everyone by bringing our own restaurant with us. We somehow pulled off the remarkable public-relations feat of operating a full-fledged restaurant serving 240 lunches a day for five days under a tent, with no kitchen, not even running water, six thousand miles away from home. We flew in the staff from California, along with California cheeses and even pots and pans. All the food was prepped in a hotel kitchen miles away and then finished off on open-air grills. A table at the California Grill was one of the toughest reservations to get in town that week. Even three-star French chefs, including Paul Bocuse and Roger Vergé came for lunch this year. It was exactly the kind of legitimizing public relations for our wines that we wanted. The credit goes to Axel Fabre, who created the California Grill. Axel runs the Great Chef's Program at Mondavi. She knows Bocuse and Vergé, and invited them personally. That day the menu was sea scallops on endive with lemon-grass butter, accompanied by Iron Horse 1987 Brut; grilled pigeon with natural gravy, roasted garlic and shiitake mushrooms and 1988 Acacia Carneros Creek Pinot Noir, and, for dessert, a sliver of rich coconut-macadamia nut tart. The ticket was $76 for two including the wines, which were all donated.

Forrest and I entertained almost every day at the Grill. The first day, we invited Olivier de la Giraudière, our primary contact at Laurent-Perrier, who distributes our wines in France. The second day, we entertained our agent for the United Kingdom, Geoffrey Roberts, who is known as "Mr. California," because he has brought quality California wines to England. The third day, we had an odd combination: our Danish agent along with a wild English trio who own and run Willi's Wine Bar—a Parisian hangout noted for its wines—Moulin au Vent, one of the best bistros in Paris, and Juvéniles, their latest venture. There wasn't enough room at the table, so Forrest had to slip away. He didn't do too badly, though: instead of a three-course meal, he had ham and cheese on a baguette at one of the cafés in the exhibition hall.

It has become a tradition for Forrest and me to co-host a dinner during Vin Expo with Martin Sinkoff, a wine importer based in Dallas who is a great taster and a great friend. Martin and I spent the first two days of Vin Expo pulling together the most interesting people we know to create an instant fête, just as if we were whipping up a soufflé. Our restaurant of choice in Bordeaux is St. James. It is the place to see and be seen. Part of the tradition is that St. James gives us the worst table in the house next to the men's room—and the worst service. Tired after a long day of promoting, Forrest was studying the wine list, looking for a white Graves to compare with our Fumé Blanc, when the sommelier, a round little man whose nickname is Doo-Doo, snatched the wine list out of his hands without taking an order, and disappeared. Thereafter, every faux pas seemed hysterically funny.

We laughed, but remained isolated, neglected, and hungry when Bocuse and Vergé graced our table, called over by one of our guests, the beautiful Françoise Parguel, a French food and wine writer who bagged Vergé as he was coming out of the men's room. After that, even Doo-Doo woke up.

Two years ago it was practically the same story, though Doo-Doo obviously didn't remember. Martin, Forrest, and I were entertaining a party of ten. Same table, same service. Jean-François Moueix sent over a magnum of château Pétrus, the rarest and most expensive red wine in the world. Jean-François is one of the most powerful wine merchants in Bordeaux, possibly in the wine world, and dangerously appealing. His family owns Pétrus. François himself, through his various outlets, dominates the international first-growth market, which operates almost like a stock exchange. The whole room turned around when the magnum was brought to us in an ice bucket. It was over 100 degrees outside and horribly humid, and even Pétrus needs to be chilled down under certain circumstances.

At our first Vin Expo, Martin got us invited to the Moueix offices at Etablissment Duclot for a first-growth tasting and buffet lunch. It was held in a stone cellar with wine crates scattered all around. Of course, they were all branded Yquem, Pétrus, and so on. A bottle of each wine was opened. Only one glass was poured for all to sip from. I hesitated, and Jean-François brought Forrest and me fresh glasses *"pour les Américains."* The French find our squeamishness about such things very amusing.

This year, we were entertained by one of the newest arrivals in Bordeaux. We were included in a dinner at a château in Entre-Deux-Mers, near the town of St. Loubé. Iron Horse, Chalone, Freemark Abbey, and Roederer Estate were invited to rub shoulders with the buyers for United and Varig airlines. We all supplied the wines. The evening was arranged by Jean Rouff, a French jet-setting entrepreneur, who brokers wine to the airlines. He divides his time between St. Tropez and Santa Fe. When he and his wife entertain, they have as many as twenty houseguests. He drives a Rolls-Royce and has his own helicopter, which he insists be flown at a height of no more than 300 feet, out of controlled air space, so he doesn't have to abide by normal flight regulations.

Our real hosts for the evening were the owners of the château, a very attractive, obviously very wealthy young couple, friends of Jean Rouff from St. Tropez. The husband made his money selling some kind of patented shaving device to Gillette. He now owns restaurants in Paris and a fleet of classic cars, and has just moved in in Bordeaux. The refurbishment of the château was a complete renovation, using the original nineteenth-century stones. Inside, all the old woodwork was stripped down to the natural pine, and they had added the most exquisite huge bathrooms and kitchen I have ever seen. There was hardly any furniture. The grounds of the château were entirely dug up. It felt as if 150 workmen had only just left. You could still smell the paint.

Our host's name was Yves. I didn't catch his last name. He looked to be about thirty-five years old, and was wearing jeans and a T-shirt, which made us feel uncomfortable because we had dressed for dinner. His wife, Catherine, who was about twenty-five, was a tiny, ethereal blonde with almost transparent skin. She had given birth to their second child just a week earlier, and was already entertaining guests. Yves took us on a tour. He has 110 acres of vineyard, 50 percent Cabernet Sauvignon and 50 percent Merlot. We couldn't see the vineyard at night, but the winery was a sight: all new equipment, everything state of the art, immaculately clean, with beautifully tiled floors and walls, computer-monitored temperature control, even stainless-steel braided hose for the refrigeration lines instead of just pipe. Such lines cost several hundred dollars a foot, and is the kind of plumbing they use on the space shuttle. And he had a full cellar of all-new oak. We tasted his first vintage, 1990, which won a gold medal in an international wine competition with 1700 entrants.

The wine was "California style," which has really now become the modern international wine style. Its emphasis is on the fruit, which makes it very tasty and remarkably approachable wine. It was eye-opening, because one rarely tastes a wine from Entre-Deux-Mers made so lavishly. By using all the technology available, Yves was able to get an enormous amount of fruit, body, and suppleness into a wine from a region that traditionally doesn't produce such interesting vintages.

Eighteen years ago, my parents asked the same question: What if you took a lower-classified château, but made the wines on the highest quality level. The classification system in Bordeaux dates to 1855, when the Châteaux in certain districts were ranked according to retail price. The best-selling wines were called the First Growths. Thereafter, it became the status quo. So far it has only been successfully challenged once, when Baron Philippe de Rothschild got Mouton elevated to the status of a first growth after a twenty-year siege.

Today, there are "superseconds" like Léoville-Las-Cases, third and even fifth growths like Lynch-Bages as well as wines like Pétrus from areas never classified that command the highest prices, but in most cases, a "lesser" château in France cannot charge much beyond its ranking and, therefore, cannot afford to incur the expense of producing higher quality—at least, not indefinitely. The oldest joke in the wine world is that the way to make a small fortune in the wine business is to start with a very large one. And trying to buck the classification is undeniably harder than starting fresh in California, where there aren't any political limitations or laws about how to make our wine.

Our last day at Vin Expo, we got a taste of the old world. We were entertained at Château Malartic-Lagravière—a classified growth that has been in one family's hands for 140 years and this year was turned over to Laurent-Perrier.

Malartic was passed down from son to son, to a daughter who died ten years ago. The founder was a seafaring merchant, who owned one of the most beautiful tall ships of the times. That ship is the emblem of the château. A model is displayed in a glass case in the living room. Mr. Marly has run the chateau since 1947. His family were industrialists; they had a mirror-manufacturing company with factories in France and Algeria. He took over the château when his father-in-law died, knowing nothing about wine making. He is now eighty years old and because his children are not independently financially capable of maintaining the château—France has very difficult laws of succession and very expensive death taxes—he was forced to sell, and chose

Bernard de Nonancourt. Mr. Marly said he had other offers, but he couldn't give Malartic to an impersonal corporation. One of Marly's sons, Bruno, will continue to work at Malartic for Laurent-Perrier. And Mr. Marly will live out his life in the château.

Lunch was in the old style—white lace tablecloth, silver trays with silver serving pieces. The first course was poached sole and foie gras, then pigeon and cèpes. This was followed by a cheese course and a very elaborate dessert: chocolate mushrooms filled with various creams. This, of course, was a working luncheon. The other guests were Laurent-Perrier's distributors from Belgium and Spain, Idaho and Puerto Rico, and the wine buyer for Air France.

We were served wines that had never moved from the cellar: a 1980 white, a 1947 red in magnum followed by their 1961, a legendary vintage. It was a tasting of our host's tenure at the château. When I thanked Mr. Marly for being so generous, he responded by quoting Omar Khayyám, "I wonder often what the Vintners buy / One half so precious as the stuff they sell."

I asked our host what allows his wine to age. He said it was the *goût du terroir*. After lunch, the old gentleman led me out into the vineyards. He bent down and picked a handful of shells out of the dirt, saying that they dated from 200,000 years ago, when the region was under the ocean. "How the wines age is somehow connected to these fossils," he said.

Sadly, this coming harvest will be one of the smallest in Bordeaux's history. Last April, a severe frost throughout France destroyed up to 80 percent of the crop in some places. Mr. Marly, Forrest, and I walked through the vineyards at Malartic, which bore so little fruit we couldn't help but be heartbroken. It was a reminder, if we ever needed one, that you can't just push a button and get a vintage.

. . .

June 26. No two people were happier to be home from France than Forrest and me. It's amazing how much changes in the vineyards and the gardens when you've been away even for a week. As soon as we arrived home, Forrest and I walked the vineyards to assess the set. The bloom is finished, the flowers have dried up and blown away, and the berries have set in loose clusters so the grapes have room to grow. The berries are pinhead to pea size, slightly oblong and bright green. If you cut one in half with your nail, there's just a little moisture inside. It has a simple, tart taste, mostly acid—no real flavor—no sugar yet. The bunches will fill out as the grapes size up. Forrest says it looks like we've got a good-size crop; he is also pleased that the vineyards at Iron Horse look very even—we counted forty clusters fairly uniformly from vine to vine. When a vineyard matures evenly, it means that our predictions for the crop will be more accurate and physically harvesting it should be easier. It is still too early to judge the intensity of the fruit.

The vines look very healthy; solid green and vigorous. The first leaves are about the size of my palm and the shoots average three feet long. In the new vineyards they look neat and tidy, held upright by experimental, multiwired trellising systems. In the original 110 acres, the vines are shooting out into the middle of the rows, so that you you have to push them aside as you walk through. It's a little jungly. When they begin cascading to the ground they will be cut back about a foot and a half, leaving just enough leaf cover to act as a parasol, so air can circulate around the grapes. The sun charges the leaves and photosynthesis makes the grapes grow.

You can detect some differences—the north-facing slopes are

more vigorous than the south-facing slopes, because they get more moisture; the rain shed tends to fall that way. The new vineyards are on drip irrigation. This is the first year the thirty-eight acres of Chardonnay and Pinot Noir planted in 1986 will be called upon to carry a full crop. They still need irrigation, some food—fertilizer and supplemental potash—and the crop may have to be thinned. The carrying capacity of a young vine is usually smaller than it is for a mature vine.

Forrest predicts—with a sigh of relief—that we could get four tons to the acre. For Father this is mixed news. We need to bring in a good-sized crop this year, and Forrest has worked very hard to get the vineyard up to this capacity. We have had such short crops the last three out of five years that our winery and man-power have been underutilized, raising our costs. A bountiful vintage would be timely to say the least, but that much of a jump from last year means we will need more stainless-steel tanks, which cost $7,500 each. They will need to be ordered by July 15 in order to be delivered by Labor Day, which will give us some time to get them installed before we start bringing in grapes. Nonetheless, with the sky so blue, the sun so bright, and a lovely breeze lowering the ambient air temperature down to 75 degrees, we can't help but feel optimistic.

Forrest and I are celebrating our first anniversary. We were married last year in an old, nearly hidden 1920s corral on our property that my parents restored for the wedding. Father planted roses all around the fence, and petunias in the old cattle chute. He laid crushed shale on the ground, and built a big, stone-covered grill on the foundation of what used to be the water trough. Outside the gate is an old rusted Model-A truck chassis, which we pulled out of the berry bushes, and an old hay rake. It is a very romantic setting. Forrest and I wanted the corral to look completely natural. But one afternoon, a few days before the wedding, we caught Mother and Father with artist-size paint brushes in hand, touching up the barn. They did a great job. No one could see the difference.

We greeted everyone with a glass of sparkling wine. There were 250 guests. I wore a dress I designed myself, using lavender and pale green silk and linen that Forrest and I had bought in Thailand and Hong Kong. My bouquet was made of the most beautiful long-stemmed roses from the garden, which Father picked and dethorned for me. We had an hour of kissing, hugging, and laughing, with fresh oysters being shucked on the far side of the barn and everyone taking photographs. Instead of a professional photographer, we passed out fling cameras—Kodak throw-away boxes—and we have dozens of pictures of people taking pictures. Finally, Forrest and I locked arms and led the crowd over to where the ceremony was going to be—no music, no procession—just our two favorite federal judges, Matt Byrne and Mariana Pfaelzer. As soon as we said our vows, the grills started sizzling.

Our chef, Mark Malicki, planned the menu three months in advance, so Father could grow all the produce. Mark spent weeks working on the logistics—making lists, lining up chefs and assistants, waiters, dishwashers—and figuring out what we needed to rent: grills, plates, a cappuccino machine. We ordered special glasses for the wedding—etched with the Iron Horse and Forrest's T-T.

Four splendid white rose trees Father had planted in cut-in-half wine barrels marked the entrance to the dining area. Everyone sat down at one long, continuous table set up on a road with vineyard on both sides and a white canopy overhead for shade. The tablecloths were pale green damask with matching napkins

T-T

Wedding Celebration
for
Joy and Forrest
Prepared by Chef Mark Malicki
June 24, 1990

In The Corral

Iron Horse 1984 Blanc de Blancs in Magnums
A selection of Hog Island Oysters with accompanying sauces
King Salmon Gravlax in two preparations
Ranch Cured Duck Prosciutto with Asian Pears

At Table

Iron Horse 1989 Fumé Blanc and Iron Horse 1982 Zinfandel
White Bean Pureé, Grilled Red Onion and Mint Salad
Barry's Salad of Mesclun and Bitter Greens
Crudités
Cracked Wheat, Onions, Parsley and Tomato Salad
with a coriander vinaigrette
A Selection of California Chevres and French Raw Milk Cheeses
Bobwhite Quail
grilled on vine canes with a tamarind, fried shallot and chili glaze
Charcoal Grilled Lamb
in a mustard herb crust with a confit of leeks
Grilled Ahi in a Black Pepper Crust
with Japanese-inspired pickled vegetables and shiso salsa
Barbecued Corn with a yellow curry basil butter
Grilled Early Summer Squash with olive oil, salt and pepper
Our First Potatoes!!

At Home

Iron Horse 1984 Late Disgorged Brut in Magnums
Assorted Berries
Wedding Cake
prepared by The American Baker Jim Dodge
Espresso and Cappuccino

that Mother had brought from France. An oak branch was tied to the back of every chair with a big white gauze bow. Mother set white petunias, geraniums, and ivy—all from Father's lath houses—down the middle of the table. By lunch, most of the men had taken off their jackets; one of my favorite pictures shows the blazers hanging in the vineyards. The joke was that you couldn't get a decent meal in most of the major cities because so many of the best chefs in America were guests at Iron Horse that day.

The quail has become one of Mark's signature dishes. Restaurateur Michael McCarty called the dish "quail in bondage," and we enjoyed it with Henry VIII gusto. The recipe has appeared in numerous newspapers and magazines, which is funny because it begins with cutting grapevine canes in February for the skewers—probably not that easy for too many people to do.

GROWTH

JULY

JULY IS A quirky month. It can be very hot, which cuts the growing season short, or it can be cool and foggy, prolonging the wait for harvest. After lunch, typically, a breeze picks up off the ocean. It feels delightfully cool on the back of your neck. By sunset there's a wall of fog looming on the southwestern horizon. In the wee hours, it marches across the property. Everything stays rather dewy until the fog retreats again at about ten o'clock. The day slowly warms up, and the vineyards will have gotten approximately ten hours of sunlight by the time the last ray of sun hits Block A at the foot of the property. The breeze and the fog refresh the vineyard. The long sunlight hours mature the fruit and bring richness to the vintage. The coolness gives our wines zest. It's the combination of the two that makes this property so interesting.

If it's hot at Iron Horse, it's really hot at T-T, at least ten degrees warmer. In the hills, though, it never gets as hot as the flatland vineyards on the valley floor. There is a cool breeze off the ocean in the evening. It is this zestiness that fine-tunes the wines from T-T to fit the Iron Horse style, which, if we were talking about music, I would describe as having more treble than bass—bright fruit and a natural liveliness in the mouth. Rich like silk as opposed to brocade. What gives our wines this character is the warmth of our days and the coolness of our nights. Such temperature swings (as much as forty degrees in a day) modulate the growth of the vine, the maturity and "character" of the fruit.

So far this summer, there has been only one day when the thermometer hit 100 degrees at Iron Horse and 110 at T-T. Otherwise it has been cool and overcast, slowing everything down. The grapes need sunshine to grow and start ripening. They are stalled again. Normally we would be getting ready for harvest by now, but Forrest is planning for a late start, spreading out the work, cutting down man hours and taking precautions against pre-harvest rain. This means plucking off leaves from the vines by hand so that, if it does rain, the fruit will dry quickly and the humidity around the clusters will be reduced. This is important to prevent rot.

The Cabernet Sauvignon is showing some signs of stress. The vines need water to support the grapes or they will shut down for self-preservation, storing their energy instead of putting out new growth. Forrest put on twenty-four hours of water, using the drip irrigation, which is the equivalent of twenty-six gallons per vine. A week later they still were not growing. He decided to overhead irrigate for twenty-four hours, hoping to stimulate a wider root area. By the last week of July, he still was not satisfied with the growth and dripped it for another twenty-four hours. There is a myth about established vineyards: that they never need irrigating and that stress is good for a vine, producing more character. It's true that too much water promotes excessive vine growth, diverting intensity away from the grapes, but vines that do not get enough water drop their leaves and the grapes never mature. To find the right balance, we use neutron probes, high-tech instruments that are driven into the ground to measure and chart how much water the vines are absorbing, but we cannot rely on technology alone. The charts have to be interpreted with the knowledge of how the vines have performed in the past and the subtleties of soil shifts throughout the vineyard.

At T-T the soil is predominantly rocky clay, becoming more eroded and meager as the land rises. At the top of the hill, the root systems are so shallow that the vines need to be tended like plants in a flowerpot. They dry out quickly, and need to be fed potash and phosphorous and watered regularly. Drip irrigation is like hand feeding, providing the amount of nourishment that each vine needs without fostering weeds between the rows.

By contrast, Iron Horse is foggy and cool—perfect for Chardonnay and Pinot Noir. The vines do not lose as much moisture through transpiration. The soils are mainly a sandy clay loam called Goldridge, with fractured shale underneath. The roots reach down eight or nine feet to available water. Here, supplemental irrigation might be detrimental to the quality of the grapes, with the exception of young vines that may need it because they do not have deeply established root systems.

Thanks to March rains, there is enough water to get us through the season, but we won't have much left over and another dry winter could be disastrous. We have to be very careful what we wish for. We want sun through harvest and then rain all winter. At the end of July, we still cannot fully assess the quality of the grapes in the vineyard. We cannot pinpoint when harvest will begin. We have a pool going in the office. The Chardonnay is still hard and green, awaiting that touch of sunshine that will turn them translucent green-gold.

At T-T things are just beginning to happen. The Sauvignon

Blanc is softening. The Cabernet Franc has one berry in a thousand changing color. The Cabernet Sauvignon is still pea sized and green. In the next week or so, Forrest must decide, before it is too late, whether to cut the canes again, which are cascading back down to the ground, and pull off more leaves and the small second crop of grapes, which are needlessly using up the vines' energy. He may even go back and thin the first crop for a second time. If a vine starts to overstress, it looks limp and the leaves start to yellow. We have to thin, or none of the grapes on that vine will mature. Thinning is a procedure Father cannot bear to watch. He leaves the property. It's like watching money drop to the ground.

Forrest walks the vineyards every day checking for wind-born mildew and pests like leafhoppers and mites. Leafhoppers suck on the juice of the leaves and render them nonfunctional for photosynthesis, arresting the maturation of the grapes. They are rarely a problem at Iron Horse. Enough of the property is left in a natural state so that there is an ecological balance between the leafhoppers and their predators. Also, Iron Horse is so isolated that we are not endangered by infestations from other vineyards. At T-T, the problem is that the Alexander Valley is warmer, and pests breed faster. The area is intensely planted to grapes—15,000 acres of vineyard—and many of the ditches and creeks have been cleaned bare of the natural habitat of the parasitic wasp, which was the natural balance to leafhoppers. And, because the vineyards are planted cheek by jowl, an infestation in one vineyard inevitably spreads to the next.

Forrest stopped using pesticides in 1988 for ecological reasons, and resorted to spraying the vines with soap, which is fairly effective if properly timed. With a pesticide you can spray any time, annihilating everything—the good bugs as well as the bad. But with biological controls, from soap sprays to releasing lacewings and ladybugs, the goal is to restore a balance so that the good bugs can do their work. Timing is crucial. There is never an immediate kill. The method usually has to be repeated a number of times, which can be frustrating and expensive. Forrest, in a cost-saving mood, has decided not to strip-spray the weeds between the vines. Weeds do not effect the growth of the vines; it's just a questions of esthetics. It will be interesting to see if he will resist spending the money, or if he will give in to the way he wants the vineyard to look.

We are totally preoccupied at the winery with bottling 1990 Chardonnay. We use traditional green Burgundy bottles, which we buy from an American glass company in Oakland. The bottles cost nine dollars a case and are delivered packed in cases of twelve—the same cases printed with our logo that we will send back out into the marketplace. Each case is upended onto a conveyor belt with a nerve-rattling crash, and the bottles, miraculously unbroken, move individually down the line. The winery crew will bottle eight hours a day, five-and-a-half days a week for four weeks. Mexican music blasts out of the radio for the whole month. Father loves the music; he finds it picturesque. Wine makers hate bottling. It subjects the wine to a traumatic mechanical process, and all kinds of things can go wrong. The machinery inevitably breaks down. Repairs have to be made while the ten people on the bottling line stand around watching. Even when the line is functioning perfectly, it bangs the wine around as it is pumped through hoses and pipes, bringing it into contact with metal parts and potentially exposing it to air. If there is a vacuum leak, oxygen will supersaturate the wine. The oxygen makes it more vulnerable to temperature swings, sunlight, and all the other bad things that can happen to a bottle of wine. We put so much faith in technology that we assume stainless-steel equipment is better than what they had in the 1800s, when cellars were full of mold and rats. They may have had some bacterial smudge in those days, but hand-filling the bottles with a siphon hose by way of gravity is still the most benign way of bottling wine. Our bottling line runs left to right. The bottles first go through a blower to rid them of dust and fiber, then they are purged with nitrogen to expel the oxygen. Within seconds, each bottle is picked up by a star wheel and moved onto the filling machine—a carousel with twelve filling tubes. A little foot raises the bottle a few inches, pushing a spring that triggers the filling tube to open. After a complete turn, the bottle is full; it is then lowered and released onto another star wheel and goes back onto the conveyor en route to the corker. You can't help but feel proud watching your bottles clink along like little soldiers. A pair of jaws take the bottle by the neck. A cork drops down into a smaller set of jaws and is squeezed to 50 percent of its diameter. A little driver comes down and knocks the cork into the bottle. The cork reexpands instantly. The corker jaws have to be perfectly aligned. If they don't squeeze together properly, the cork will crease, allowing oxygen to seep into the wine, or, if the crease is very deep, actually letting the wine leak out. The quality of the cork is very important to how the wine ages. A perfect cork is odorless and uniformly dense. The best come from Portugal, and are made from the bark of cork trees which are peeled once every ten years, then air dried for another two years. We pay thirty cents apiece for extra-select quality corks. Even then, we routinely reject 10 percent.

After corking, the bottle travels three feet down the line to a person who drops a foil capsule in its noncompressed form onto the top of the bottle. It sits there like a little hat. The bottle goes up into the foiler, where eight rollers spin the little foil hat tightly onto the neck of the bottle. We use 100 percent tin capsules on our wine bottles, not lead. Tin is less malleable than lead, so we had to buy a new machine, tear apart our bottling line, take out the old foiler, replace it with the new one and add twenty feet of conveyor. Tin floats on the commodities market, and our first order cost fifteen cents apiece, twice what lead capsules cost. But by January 1, 1992, lead will be banned from landfills in ten states.

The labeling machine is the most complex of all. It orients the bottle into position, applies glue to a label, and then the label onto the bottle. The biggest problem is that the label is apt to be crooked. The labeler goes in and out of sync endlessly. It is loaded with cams and gears and requires an enormous amount of tinkering. The slightest thing can throw it into a tizzy. You might walk in and the place will look as if it has been papered with labels, because the machine is spewing them out and spitting glue everywhere.

Shirley Everly, who is in charge of quality control, stands there and makes sure the labels are on straight. Everybody says, "Looks okay to me." And Shirley says, "Nope, it's crooked." And John or Andrew has to realign the machine. They are the only two who can make it work. And Shirley cracks the whip: "It is not good enough, stop! Fix it again." If Forrest walks in and sees the thing misperforming, his immediate reaction is to walk out. He can't fix it. He wouldn't know where to begin. Andrew takes great pride in being able to have his way with the machine.

We regularly overfill our bottles. A bottle is supposed to

contain 750 ml. But we fill to 760 ml so there is less space for oxygen between the wine and the cork. Most premium wineries overfill and have to file a form with the Bureau of Alcohol, Tobacco and Firearms accounting for every milliliter for tax reasons. We pay the government .34 cents per gallon on still wine and $3.60 for sparkling.

One of the most agonizing aspects of wine making is designing the label, creating the whole package, coming up with a name, a logo, an image. There are professionals who do these things. Many wineries do it themselves. More often than not, it's a little bit of both. Our label is practically our only form of merchandising—that and our pricing.

Our sparkling wine labels are gray with silver pinstripes wrapping around the bottle, and with the rampant horse embossed in silver. The vintage changes every year, so we constantly have the opportunity or obligation to revise our image. We have been using the same design for the sparkling for ten years. It's time for a change. We are influenced by one of my father's friends, a business consultant named Ben Heirs, who has written a fascinating book called *The Professional Thinker*. His theory is that evolution in all things is essential. He has recommended updating our package to be "20–30 percent more eyecatching," but still recognizable. In the meantime, Gary Fishman, who works at Wally's Liquors in Los Angeles, pointed out that our sparklings all look alike—that our Wedding Cuvée, for example, carries the same label as our Brut, except for the name. We are working on a design that will distinguish each one, but also form a collection or family of Iron Horse sparklings that will give the retailer a reason to put them all on the shelf together.

Wine labels have to be approved every year, even if all we are changing is the vintage and some general descriptive material about the wine. Label approval falls under the supervision of the BATF—Bureau of Alcohol, Tobacco and Firearms. Tough crowd. They always make me think about the revenue agents who busted up moonshiners and bootleggers in the twenties and early thirties. My Grandpa Dave drank champagne served in coffee cups at the Deauville Club in Santa Monica all through Prohibition. I joke with my mother that if Prohibition comes back, she'll take care of the medicinal and religious end of the business and I'll be the rumrunner.

A great deal of the information on the label is mandated by the federal government. The label has to give the alcohol content, the appellation of origin, the government warning about alcohol, and the "contains sulfites" warning. "Grown, Produced and Bottled," "Estate Bottled" or "Proprietor Grown" means that the winery grew the grapes, made the wine, and bottled it. "Produced and Bottled" means the winery bought the grapes. Sometimes the specific vineyard is indicated. This is a mark of quality going back to the time of the pharaohs. Archeologists have deciphered names and dates on the wine jars buried in ancient tombs. "Vinted" or "Made and Bottled" or just "Bottled by" means that the wine was bought in bulk or was produced at another bonded winery.

Most wines now have Universal Product Codes—even Dom Pérignon Champagne has the bar code, which can be scanned electronically. A UPC code used to mean "supermarket wine." Now we're all fighting to sell to upscale supermarkets like Safeway and Vons Pavillions in California, mainly because the volume is so great.

The BATF has the authority to disallow any label it doesn't approve of. Clos Pegase wanted to reproduce one of the paintings in their collection—a very famous Dubuffet. The government decided it was sexually explicit and made them edit the painting. We've been advised that two of our sparkling labels have to change or they will be disallowed because they're too shiny. Their letter says the glare makes it too difficult to read the mandatory information. Sometimes I think there is a certified blind person in the inspection department who seems to have only one stamp: REJECT. In the old days, if they disapproved but the labels were already printed, you could get a use-up. Now we can't do that anymore. They routinely throw back labels if even a comma is missing in the government warning.

July 20. At the end of each day, Father, Laurence, Forrest and I go down to the garden and pick to our heart's content. We never seem to make a dent in it. Two or three times a week Mark prepares nine-course vegetarian meals. He gets such a kick out of it because his expenses—what he has to go out and buy from a store—rarely exceed $1.50. The lettuce is so prolific that we only take the center leaves, and we can pick any size squash we want. Keeping up with the squash is the challenge.

The corn is knee high. There is plenty of lettuce and we have our first squash. This is a time when zucchini tastes delicious, before the novelty wears off and there is such an overabundance that you cannot give it away. Strawberries border the walkways around the big house. We can pick them early in the morning for breakfast, but they are better at the end of the day when they are warm and taste like freshly made jam. We are harvesting beets—red beets, golden beets, candy-striped, and pure white beets—which do beautifully in our sandy soil. Contrary to most vegetables, they taste sweeter as they get bigger.

. . .

We started selling vegetables commercially two years ago. No family could possibly consume the quantities Father has planted. When he shows off his gardens to the top chefs who come to visit the winery, they all want to buy from him. Sadly, it has not turned out to be a viable enterprise. The cost of producing perfect vegetables far exceeds the market value. Also, Father is reluctant to part with some of his rare items. The San Francisco restaurant Postrio once wanted to buy all of his Romanesco broccoli—or none—but Father would not sell it to them because he did not want to be deprived. On the other hand, it pains him to see it go to waste. It seems that each week, at every meal, we have a particular vegetable prepared every conceivable way. Nothing infuriates him more than when we buy produce from a store, even avocados or bananas, which we can't grow ourselves.

This month, we have successfully demolished the fingerling potatoes, the peas, a full bed of carrots. Thankfully, the remaining fava beans were plowed under in June and the artichokes have already flowered.

July 20. Berries love our weather. There is a big banner over the Green Valley Blueberry Farm sign, right before you get to Iron Horse, gleefully announcing THE BERRIES ARE IN! Everybody is excited. People drive from all over to buy directly from the farms around us. We grow our own. Father has planted a berry-lover's fantasy: row after row of blueberries and raspberries, each a different size, color, flavor, with different degrees of sweetness and tartness. The golden raspberries are the ultimate luxury. They have a shelf life of about two hours. My favorites are the small, very crunchy, seedy Black Caps. The wild blackberries are slowly ripening. We have five acres of wild blackberries on the property, and what looks like a huge crop this year.

All the berries here have an intensity that's very hard to find when you buy them from a store. Half the pleasure is picking them yourself, eating them as you go. It takes over an hour to fill a flat. Father takes his granddaughters, Justine and Barrie, picking. They get purple stains on their hands and faces and we all eat berries and cookies at almost every meal for dessert. Forrest and I spill a heap of them on pound cake and spoon on a little berry-and-yogurt sauce. When I'm feeling extravagant, I drop a handful into a glass of sparkling wine, and for me there is probably nothing better than fresh berries and cereal for breakfast.

All the berry patches, as well as the fruit trees, are netted. As a concession to the birds, Father planted two mulberry trees, hoping they would leave the rest of the fruit alone. Of course it didn't work, so we get back at the birds by eating the mulberries, too. We used to sell our wild blackberries through a broker who shipped all over the United States, but it didn't pay. We would have been happy to break even, but the sale of the berries couldn't cover the cost of picking them.

For Forrest's fortieth birthday a few years ago, we rented a hot-air balloon to take off from our house. There were eight of us, so we had to go in two shifts, but that wasn't a problem because the balloon ride comes with a "chase car," so we could take turns. One thing about ballooning is you can control where you take off but not necessarily where you land.

The balloonists—a gray-haired character and a couple of kids he had working for him—arrived at 6:00 A.M. We got to help them unfold the balloon, and we stood outside in the cold and fog for hours while they linked all the ropes to the basket and pumped the balloon full of hot air. The take-off was just like going up in an elevator. It was a slow ascent and the gondola felt very solid underfoot. It was quiet and warm from the periodic blasts of hot air. The thrill was getting a real bird's-eye view of Iron Horse. From overhead it looks really quite big.

Our first stop was in an open field in Sebastopol, which was a little tricky because of the telephone wires; our second flight headed southwest—toward Petaluma and the ocean. The balloon cast this great shadow and the *whoosh* of the steam spooked all the farm animals. It hits some frequency that drives them crazy—the dogs start barking and the cows get so upset they could easily run right into a fence and hurt themselves. The farmer whose property we landed on wasn't the least bit amused. He ran out of his house bare chested to yell at us for stirring up his cattle. As we were leaving, I noticed a big sign near the farmer's gate stating that it was a future development site for tract housing.

Normally this would be the time when the balloonist provides a bottle of sparkling wine, but under the circumstances the "chase car" took us home. Our friend Dean Fearing, chef of the Mansion on Turtle Creek in Dallas, started describing what he would make for the ultimate Iron Horse post-ballooning breakfast: eggs, salsa, corn bread, Babcock peaches right off the tree, and, of course, Brut. By the time we got back to our house it was 10:00 A.M. and we were famished, so we gave Dean about twenty minutes to get everything on the table.

Most of the vineyards in Sonoma were formerly fruit orchards, dairies, or berry farms. The Alexander Valley was planted to prunes and walnuts when Forrest's parents bought T-T in 1950.

One of their neighbors, Robert Young, was the best prune grower in the area. Forrest's father had about fifteen acres, but the prune business wasn't doing very well, leaving Forrest, Sr., a San Francisco financier, to wonder what he was going to do with so many prunes. He and Bob Young would talk about the problem long into the night. At the time, Forrest's father had fallen in love with serving a Polish plum brandy called slivovitz to his guests as an after-dinner drink. And it didn't take too many shots of it before they came up with the idea of making Sonomavitz as a play on words and as a way to use the prunes. Fortunately, Bob Young started planting Cabernet Sauvignon instead, and Forrest's father followed suit.

The Sebastopol area used to be famous for the Gravenstein apple. Today, this is practically an heirloom variety. Primarily a baking apple, it will probably never come back as an industry. During the 1970s, the county let the second- and third-generation apple growers subdivide their orchards with little consideration as to how it would affect agriculture. The result is a tug-of-war between developers and farmers over the land's potential as vineyard or orchard because of its ever-increasing real estate value.

All around us more and more houses are being built. Our neighbors regularly complain about anything we spray on the vineyards, and about tractor noise before dawn. It's as if they moved to the country and then the first thing they want to get rid of *is* the country. One woman came pounding on our door while we were still getting dressed demanding to know what we were putting on the roses alongside our house. I was furious and wanted to tell her it was none of her business. In fact, Forrest uses sulfur and seaweed on the roses, just as he does on the vines, but there was this insinuation that we must be doing something bad. At the last county-planning board meeting, another neighbor made an impassioned speech about our deer fence around the new vineyard on Thomas Road, which she said looked like a concentration camp and impeded the free movement of wildlife. Wait until she sees the bird cages we erect during harvest to trap the linnets when they come home to roost! The birds pick at the grapes, draining the juice. We used to broadcast canned distress signals and shotgun blasts at dawn and dusk, from huge loudspeakers hung on the telephone poles, but that drove everybody crazy. Now we lure the birds into cages with seed to break their nesting and feeding patterns, and then turn them over to the state. We don't discuss what happens to them.

The wildlife—the birds and the deer especially—are charming and decorative, humorously annoying or painfully destructive depending on your perspective. The strangest is the family of linnets that nest every spring in the parlor chimney at my parents' house. The other day we went into the parlor after lunch for coffee with Lindsay Wurlitzer, the loan officer from Production Credit. We were just about to get down to business when the sound of chirping birds came floating out of the fireplace. It was impossible to keep a straight face. And Father has an ongoing war with the deer. We have a deer fence tucked away in the overgrowth out of sight, but the deer just get through it. They eat the young shoots off his vines, his vegetables, and his roses. I must say the way they chomp on a grapevine or ravage a rose bush does make you want to cover your eyes in horror, and they brazenly come right up to the house. Mark was once embarrassed in the middle of an interview for *Market Watch* magazine when a deer stole his focaccia right off the luncheon table.

We won a modicum of satisfaction last fall. Forrest came

home one morning and yelled, "Honey, it's me. I'm just changing my pants. I got blood all over them." I thought, "Okay, I'll
bite," and asked, "What happened?" Apparently a deer had
become trapped inside the fence on Thomas Road. It was
wounded, so we shot it and Forrest had brought it down to
Mark. Mark let it hang in Father's wine room for a week and
prepared the most tender venison imaginable—which was not
surprising considering the deer had eaten nothing but radicchio,
roses, and grapes.

At least it was deer season.

Normally, we do not allow any hunting on the property—
there are too many households with children for it to be safe—so
we rely on Matt, one of the federal judges who married Forrest
and me, to bring us wild game when he comes to visit. Last
weekend he arrived with a freezer load of duck. Mark prepared
duck three ways: duck ravioli in broth, roasted duck breast, and
then warm duck cracklings spooned out of the pan onto fresh
baby greens. Mother said it was one of the best meals she has ever
had. We drank a bottle of our 1980 Chardonnay with the first
course. It was a perfect combination. The wine when it was
poured was very intense in color, not the pale green-gold of
young wines, but solid gold—almost amber, like sherry, but not
brown; browning definitely means that a wine is heading over
the hill. It was luscious, rich, round, heavily textured without
being cloying, still refreshing, inviting another sip. It had a
slightly syrupy quality—probably due to the alcohol. Alcohol
can give a perception of sweetness and it gives weight to wine.
All of the best, most long-lived Chardonnays and Pinot Noirs,
wherever they're made in the world, have a relatively high
alcohol—13 to 14 percent. It's part of what preserves them.

Father had chilled a second bottle, which turned out to be the same vintage but barrel fermented. My parents preferred it; I thought it was overly oaky; Forrest thought the bottle was corked, which means that the cork was flawed and the wine had picked up some off odors and flavors; this doesn't necessarily make the wine bad—in a technical sense, corkiness is a fault, but it can come across as a degree of complexity that may be pleasing. Corkiness can run the gamut from woody, earthy, or mushroomy, to moldy, funky, or just plain off. One person's corkiness may be another person's pleasure, and while Forrest as a wine maker may be very unforgiving, flaws can be as appealing in wines as they are in people. We all taste differently, and part of the fun is trying to describe smells and tastes. It's a wonderful playing field for the intellect—like lying on your back on the grass as a kid, identifying the shapes in the clouds. There are no wrong answers. For some reason, one of the hardest things to do with wine is to just open and taste it, to think of it as a sensory experience, even a sensual one. It does after all contain a known aphrodisiac—alcohol. Or maybe it's just talking about it that's hard. At a tasting for an ophthalmology convention in San Francisco, an eye doctor asked me to describe the color of our Cabernet. I wanted to shoot back, "Red, for starters," but he was in earnest. He just wanted a vocabulary with which to describe the wine to someone else. At least he recognized gradations of red.

Smells are even harder to describe, and Forrest says 90 percent of wine is smell. Most of the problem comes down to finding adjectives and metaphors; and having a wine described to you by a really great taster—someone who's experienced and articulate—is like having an expert describe a painting. It can be quite poetic, or it can be obtuse. Some experts use intensely personal experiences to describe wine, which makes it impossible to know what they're talking about. André Tchelistcheff is famous for saying California Cabernet is like a young woman wrapped in fur, and Michael Broadbent says there is a quality he looks for in Burgundies which remind him of walks on the beach in Bristol, England.

More often than not, winespeak is merely pretentious and boring. The classic is the James Thurber cartoon for *The New Yorker* showing a wine snob addressing a wine: "It's a naïve, domestic Burgundy without any breeding, but I think you'll be amused by its presumption." More recently, *The New Yorker* had a cartoon about another kind of wine bore droning on "You know, I paid, $40 for that Lafite in 1974," while his dinner partner drifts off to sleep.

Tasting with a wine maker, however, shows that the whole tasting game shouldn't be taken too seriously. I was once at a Pinot Noir tasting with five wine makers. It was for the Buyers' Circle—a consortium of heavy-hitting New York restaurateurs and members of the East Coast media who each paid $55 for their own lunch and the chance to taste selected wines on a monthly basis. Most of the buyers in the group don't see salesmen anymore, so this was a rare opportunity to get them to taste our wine.

The tasting started at 11:00 A.M. sharp, and the rules were that the wine makers were not allowed to interfere with the tasters because we would cut into their allotted forty-five minutes of tasting time before lunch and talking to us might unduly influence their feelings about a wine, good or bad.

The wine makers and I were put at a table all by ourselves. Our places were set with five glasses and the wines were already poured. We tasted, took notes, but didn't really comment on the wines, which was surprising since they had been served in reverse order. This was not a blind tasting—we knew, or thought

we knew, which order the wines had been poured, but wine
makers are used to tasting left to right, that's the way they are
poured in a tasting room—whereas a restaurateur would always
pour right to left, following normal table service. Josh Jensen in
the middle couldn't miss identifying his wine, but the others—
David Graves, David Adelsheim, Mike Richmond, and Forrest—never mentioned any confusion, which led me to
conclude that they were either hungover, simply not paying
attention, or extremely well mannered. You'd think one of
them would say "Gee . . . this doesn't taste like my wine."

Many people say they can't tell the difference between one
wine and another, but when I take them into the orchard to taste
an array of peaches or plums, they can easily taste the variations
from one to the next. If they'd relax, they would be able to do
the same with wine. This whole place is an object lesson about
diversity—from the roses to the berries to the wines.

Late July is when people we know go to "The Grove." A good
friend used to go quite often. He probably would have been
there this summer were it not for Forrest. The Bohemian Grove,
ten miles from us, is where members of San Francisco's Bohemian Club, captains of industry and high government officials,
fly in on private jets to rough it in the woods. During the six
weeks that the Grove is open, Santa Rosa Municipal Airport
looks like Aspen International. It's entertainment for the locals
to watch the G2s and G3s take off and land. Demonstrations,
protesting one thing or another, are always going on outside its
gates. The Grove itself is so beautiful it could easily qualify as a
State Park. It's amazing that it's a private club, though it can be
argued that being private is what has saved it.

Henry Kissinger is a regular. Ronald Reagan was there this

year. For security reasons, a sitting president is never invited. It's like summer camp, where the top men in the country can act like boys, replete with campfires, barbecues, and sing-alongs, all in the complete privacy of a huge redwood forest. Women are excluded even as waitresses. Two generations ago, the oil tycoons would come back from The Grove and tell my grandfather, an independent oil man, what he could charge for gasoline. He had a small chain of gas stations in Southern California called Eagle Oil. Of course, he didn't comply, and he was squeezed out of the business.

Last year we were invited to a birthday party at The Grove on a special night when women would be allowed. Three members pulled their weight to arrange it. There were twenty of us. It seemed as though we had the encampment to ourselves except for the guard at the gate who directed us where to park, and the driver who took us to our site. It was made very plain that the women had to be out by 9:00 P.M., or, as the guard said, "The trees would fall down."

Mystery surrounds The Grove. Most people assume that pretty heavy drinking goes on there and our party was no exception. Toward the end of the evening, the toasts began. Forrest's was unforgettable. "As a child of the sixties," he said, "I can't believe the women here tonight are allowing themselves to be bamboozled by the power and privilege associated with being at The Grove. The redwoods here are just like redwoods anywhere else and we all know that the only reason anyone comes here is to piss on trees."

Father put his head in his hands. Mother stared at Forrest in disbelief, "He couldn't have said that, could he?" and the friend whose birthday we were celebrating claims he didn't hear the toast at all. It will be a while before we are invited back. One of the hosts was put on probation for having too many guests. To his credit, he wrote a protest letter saying he felt he was being singled out for his liberal position on admitting women.

Forrest is constantly monitoring the strength of the vines to make sure they make it through to a late harvest. He continues watering, which is practically sacrilegious this late in the year. "What else is there to do?" he says stoically. "I can't fly over the property with a sun lamp—and I can't shield it with an umbrella." Ironically, his main concern is water. About 3000 gallons of water a day are being used in the gardens. Forrest says he has never seen the reservoir so low. But it's worth it. I have never tasted such sweet fruit and vegetables. There's an intensity of flavor and firmness of texture as well as abundance that is quite reassuring. There's no reason to believe that the same won't be true in the vineyards. It is a golden rule, as with any fruit or vegetable, that the longer the grapes stay on the vine, the more character they will develop.

July 28. Just as we were walking out the door this morning, David Berkeley, a Sacramento wine merchant and unofficial wine advisor to the White House, called, asking that we send two cases of sparkling wine to Washington immediately, to be loaded onto Air Force One. It had to be something very special and it had to be tomorrow: the president was going to Moscow for the signing of the START treaty and he was going to toast the achievement with Iron Horse.

Fortunately, Raphael was just labeling another batch of "pink line" Brut at the winery. It's a special cuvée that Forrest designed for the Lark Creek Inn, using our 1987 Brut and a Brut Rosé dosage. At Bradley Ogden's suggestion, Forrest made it a little sweeter so it could go with certain desserts, which also makes it a perfect toasting wine. We call it "pink line" here at the winery because the only difference in the package is a thin pink line that runs through the body label.

Sending wine for the White House requires some concern for security. We were asked to airfreight two cases to be held for pickup by the Secret Service at Dulles Airport. Nowhere on the shipping tags should it give the wine's destination. We're just supposed to call the chief usher at the executive mansion with the flight, time of arrival, and air bill number.

It's ironic that liberal Democrats like us would do so well with the Republicans in power. The Reagan administration brought Iron Horse to prominence by serving our sparkling wine at the Geneva and Washington, D.C., summits with Mikhail Gorbachev. And now, on July 31, Iron Horse will be part of the crowning moment of the Bush-Gorbachev summit in Moscow. This is a dramatic change from when the Democrats were in power. Father took me to a lunch at the White House during the Carter administration, and we were served iced tea. Before that, when California's wineries were in their infancy, the Kennedys served nothing but French wines.

Getting out a press release about an event like this is a massive amount of work. We were on the phone all day to our contacts in the media, but we had to be careful because the White House imposes an embargo on publicizing such events until after the dinner takes place. Then the White House itself releases the menu, including the wines. *The New York Times* reprinted the menu and *Time* magazine carried the story in its Business Notes section. That Monday morning, the White House called asking for an invoice as soon as possible, which, of course, we would not send. Having our wine served at the summit meeting is a connection with an historic event, and whatever your politics, it's impressive to have your wine selected for such an august occasion. It is also a public-relations coup. We printed up point-of-sale material—shelf talkers to be posted in retail stores across the country—practically taking credit for the signing of the START treaty. As fate would have it, the shelf talkers went out the day the coup started in the Soviet Union. Briefly, it seemed as though our fortunes—or at least our bragging rights—would rise or fall with Gorbachev. We sold 1000 cases of that wine in two weeks. We normally sell 500 cases of Brut per month.

AUGUST

Normally harvest begins the last few days of August, but at this point it feels like it may never happen. The weather is cold and dreary. We wake up to fog every morning. We're lucky if the sun breaks through by noon. It even rained one day—August 2—which fortunately turned out to be a nonevent. Forrest and I surveyed the property in the Land Cruiser at sunset. It was a perfect evening. A rosy pink light made the reeds in the reservoir seem surreal. The ground was already dry. There was no humidity; just a gentle breeze, no damage.

The next morning, thunderstorms were predicted. The sky was threatening, but holding. A San Francisco reporter called to set up a live shot for the six o'clock news, if it started to rain. Fortunately, no news. I tried to talk her into a human-interest story on the wait and the worry, but only destruction would do. "Call me if it rains," she said.

. . .

Chicago in August may not sound like a holiday, but the city was unseasonably cool and breezy and Charlie Trotter was celebrating the fourth anniversary of the opening of his restaurant. It was a special occasion. Charlie's a friend. There was absolutely nothing to do in the vineyards. The food was great and Forrest and I have no qualms traveling two thousand miles for a party, especially when they're serving our wines.

Joachim Splichal of Patina flew in from Los Angeles to co-chef the feast. There were pounds of caviar, truffles, and foie gras. No expense was too great. The scallops cost $5 apiece wholesale and were still wiggling when they were delivered to the restaurant.

It was going on midnight when we sat down to eat, most of the paying guests had gone home, and Charlie, Joachim and Charlie's sous-chef, could get out from behind the stove. Other chef friends from around town joined in as their restaurants closed. It amazes me how chefs can feast this way at any time of day or night.

No one batted an eye at red wine with fish. The standout favorite was our Fumé Blanc with the tuna tartar. Not an easy match, because of the coriander in the dish. For the finale, instead of the fruit listed on the menu, Charlie sent out fourteen desserts, which we passed around the table so we could taste them all.

August 12. *The Press Democrat* in Santa Rosa ran a story in the business section on the lateness of the harvest and potential disaster. Rodney Strong was quoted as saying it was the coldest season in twenty years. After that, a man stopped Forrest in the bank to say how sorry he was that we'd lost our crop.

Handwritten inscriptions surrounding the menu:

Thank you for all the wines + all the memories — Joy Sterling

Your wonderful — Tony Terlato

Larry Stone

When I drink your wine, it's like emerging from the thickets of the wild... and into the open air... Forget it — I'm drunk! — [signature]

Thanks for supporting my wacky restaurant with your great wines!! charlie

Joy to Moscow
Joy to chicago
Joy to the world!
Best —
Bill Rice

Joy! Wine is Life

Couronnes & Côtes
Roland

Thank you for sending us Gorgeous folks!

Vive le Chocolat
MaryBeth Liccioni

CHARLIE TROTTER'S

Charlie Trotter's Fourth Anniversary Dinner
August 5th and 6th, 1991

Joachim B. Splichal, Patina
Joy Sterling and Forrest Tancer, Iron Horse Vineyards

* * *

Amuse Bouche
(Oyster & Sevruga Caviar en Gelee with Nasturtium-Citrus Oil)
Iron Horse Blanc de Blanc 1986

* * *

Spicy Tuna Tartare & Tomato Fondant with Chilled Coriander Broth
Iron Horse Fume Blanc 1990

* * *

Pile of Crisp Potatoes with Sea Scallops & Osetra Caviar
Iron Horse Chardonnay 1988 (Magnum)
Joachim B. Splichal

* * *

Maine Lobster with Young Leeks & Summer Truffles (Truffle Juice & Olive Oil)
Iron Horse Chardonnay "Special Lot" 1987
Joachim B. Splichal

* * *

Seared Raw Salmon & Crispy Somen Noodles with Red Wine-Foie Gras-Wild Mushroom Essence
Iron Horse Pinot Noir "Reserve" 1986 (Magnum)

* * *

Polenta of Sturgeon with Apple Smoked Bacon
Iron Horse Cabernet Sauvignon 1982 (Magnum)
Joachim B. Splichal

* * *

Desserts
("Fruit !! Give me Fruit!! Always Fruit!!")
Iron Horse "Pink Line" Brut 1987

* * *

Petits Fours

In fact, we are nowhere near ready to jump off a bridge. If we get an Indian summer, this could turn out to be an exceptional vintage. It's traditional for the hottest time of the year to be when kids go back to school. Forrest says he remembers much cooler summers than this, though that was in the fifties. We expect to hand out sweatshirts to teeth-chattering guests, tell them how good the cold is for the grapes, and quote Mark Twain, who said, "The coldest winter I ever spent was a summer in San Francisco."

All the talk about a rivalry between Napa and Sonoma is absolutely true. It's like Bordeaux and Burgundy. Tuscany and Piemonte. Naturally, we think Sonoma is the best.

It just rankles when someone says Napa or "the valley" when they mean wine country in general. We never go to Napa unless we are invited. Forrest always tells people that they ask for our passports at the county line. Besides, it's a long drive from Iron Horse and the summer traffic is terrible.

Generally speaking, Sonoma is much cooler than Napa, which is why we are able to make much more elegant, refined wines. T-T is only fifteen miles north of the Napa line, which shows how far east it is and how warm compared to Iron Horse. But it's still this side of the hill and high enough up to get a breeze off the ocean. Sonoma is much more spread out than Napa. Much more real. Napa is kind of a theme park. They have more phoney châteaux than we do, and most of the wineries are lined up one after another on Highway 29. There is a Wine Train which takes tourists up and down that one row. This train is the source of continuous bickering among the Napa vintners. Some are vehemently opposed because it's too touristy. Others are upset because the people don't get off the train to spend money in the wineries themselves. Most Sonomans don't give the Wine Train much thought, though this summer a wine maker from our side of the mountain, Jim Bundschu, boarded the train Jessie James-style—on horseback and wearing a bandanna—and started pouring Sonoma wines for the passengers.

Both counties can be accused of being provincial—for only serving local wines. Table 29, near the town of Napa, caused a sensation throughout wine country by daring to feature a French wine: $8.50 a glass for Veuve Cliquot, which happens to be one of the very few champagne firms that doesn't have property in California.

The differences between Napa and Sonoma really shine at our respective charity wine auctions. Napa's takes place in June, ours in mid-August. Both stem from the Hospice de Beaune Auction in Burgundy. The Napa Wine Auction is a $400 ticket for a full weekend of black-tie affairs centered around their main auction at Meadowood Resort. The Sonoma package costs less, but we think it is much more fun. Our main event takes place under a big pink tent on the front lawn of the Sonoma Mission Inn.

Lunch is set up like a farmer's market, with the most exotic vegetables, farm cheeses, country breads, grilled Sonoma baby lamb, Sonoma sausages, and locally raised quail and rabbit. The tables and chairs are under the tent so eating won't interfere with bidding. We always sit right in front.

Our auctioneer, Fritz Hatton, president of the wine department of Christie's, New York, is, in comparison with Napa's auctioneer, absolutely wild. Fritz starts his auctions with stretching exercises, "Bid, Bid, Bid," he intones. "Let me see those paddles. Higher. Higher." He routinely accepts bids after the hammer falls. He mercilessly teases anyone who tries to exercise spousal restraint and he actively encourages people to bid against themselves. This is for charity, and it's fun except for that short excruciating time when our own lots are on the block.

As irrational as it may seem, we take the auction seriously. Like most of the other principals, we carry out our own lots when they come up in the auction, exposing ourselves to potential humiliation during the bidding. It's embarrassing standing there holding up a bottle and feeling like Vanna White while our reputation is being judged by how much money our items generate.

The Napa event is even more competitive. The story is that Robert Mondavi gave the shirt off his back to get Napa's final tally over $1 million. The Sonoma auction raised about half that. Ours is a much smaller, friendlier event. Four hundred or so people compared to 1400. Besides, we're told that for the Napa Valley Wine Auction the chefs import all their produce from Sonoma.

It seems we spent an inordinate amount of time blending the 1989 Cabernets. I don't know why it was such a tussle. Maybe because we have so much time on our hands waiting for harvest. We had six lots of Cabernet Sauvignon and four lots of Cabernet Franc. They were all lovely wines, but everything together tasted muddled. We blended, tasted, reblended, tasted and, after much trial and error, narrowed our options to two favorites. We ended up making both. Lot #1 is 70 percent Cabernet Sauvignon and 30 percent Cabernet Franc. Lot #2 has 26 percent Cabernet Franc. Such decisions are purely subjective. We simply make the wines we like best, the ones that keep popping up as the favorites in the tastings. Calling one #1 and the other #2 was just a guess. We wait a year after bottling before we release red wine, in order to give it some age. It will be interesting to see which one we send out first.

The idea of blending instead of planting just one grape is to have more notes to play with. You don't want to junk it up, so you let a blend build slowly. In that sense, it is very painterly, building up layers like glazing. The goal is to achieve a silky texture and as much complexity as possible so that the wine has depth. Also, each glass should tell a story. It should have a beginning, a middle, and an end. Blending is very cerebral. Even after deciding what to plant, you still have to wait four years for a crop, plus two years while the wine is in barrel. That gives you plenty of time to think about it.

Forrest made 100 percent Cabernet Sauvignon off T-T from 1978 to 1984. In 1982, he t-budded or regrafted four acres of Zinfandel on his property to Cabernet Franc, which cut down the wait. He was able to attempt his first blend in 1985. And now that he's finding his stride with it, the wine is going through a whole new metamorphosis with the addition of Sangiovese, which Forrest planted in 1988. He keeps telling me "Change is good."

The hallmark of Cabernet Sauvignon from the Alexander Valley is its bright, plummy, soft, berry character. It is typically quite tasty and approachable when young. The interesting thing is that if you try to make it "bigger," more tannic, the result can be bitter or harsh. Forrest's goal is to make a wine that combines the lusciousness of the Alexander Valley with more muscle and complexity, more definition and more facets. It is a wine that hasn't been made yet—a new taste he is still working to achieve.

Forrest took a chance on Cabernet Franc because he felt it was going to be more interesting than Merlot at T-T. Adding Merlot, a more common blending grape, to our Cabernet would have been like putting fruit on top of fruit. Also, the two grapes mature at different rates in the bottle. Merlot ages more quickly—which led Forrest to believe that the blend would fall apart with time. He picked Cabernet Franc to fill out the middle of the wine—give it more structure, backbone, and stateliness, as well as some spice—a kind of a peppery-smoky character. There was hardly any Cabernet Franc grown in California that Forrest could taste, and nothing could tell him how it would express itself at T-T. He had to extrapolate from all he knew about Bordeaux, the Loire, and his own property. Even before he got his first crop, he planted a few more acres just because he thought the ground looked right for it.

While he was composing the wine in his mind, he assumed he was going to add only 5 to 10 percent. But in the tastings, it didn't work out that way. Our favorite blend of 1985 was 72 percent Cabernet Sauvignon and 28 percent Cabernet Franc—3 percent over the legal limit of how much you can add and still call your wine Cabernet Sauvignon. We were required to give it a proprietary name and came up with "Cabernets" to signify the two types of Cabernet—Cabernet Sauvignon and Cabernet Franc in the blend. The percentages change each vintage based solely on what makes the best wine. During the first few years, Forrest gradually increased the amount of Cabernet Franc to over 30 percent. More recently he has backed off to about 26 to 27 percent. We learned from making sparkling that fractions can make a huge difference in a wine.

Next month, we will harvest our first crop of Sangiovese, the principal grape from Italy. Sangiovese is a grape that goes back to the Etruscans. It is native to Italy. There are 200,000 acres of it all over Italy, though the greatest Sangiovese-based wines come from Tuscany. In the past five years several hundred acres have been planted in California. Some of the wines that have been released already are Robert Pepi, Atlas Peak, which was instigated by Piero Antinori, and Chianti Station from Seghesio.

Sangiovese has what enologists call a fingerprint—certain flavor descriptors that fit that particular grape. It's cherry, raspberry, plum, violet, cranberry, blackberry, some citrus, peach, pear—not the fruit, but eau de vie—banana. Black tea leaves, pepper wood, honey, juniper, pine, and underbrush. It's generally firm and crisp in the mouth. It has good acidity, medium color, and medium tannins. It's kind of a younger brother to Cabernet Sauvignon.

Again there is very little planted in California, and nothing that can duplicate what T-T will yield. All we know is that we love the cherry-cranberry quality of the Sangiovese blends from Tuscany, and we think the grape will be a more sophisticated version of our red Zinfandel.

Forrest's idea is to move beyond the grapes we originally planted, not so as to be just new and different, but to light upon a style that is all our own. In the late sixties, everyone wanted to emulate the great European wines. Chardonnay, Cabernet Sauvignon, Sauvignon Blanc, Riesling, and Pinot Noir predominated. That was the fashion. They were considered the best grapes in the world and commanded the highest prices. There were a few hold-over vineyards of Zinfandel and oceans of less expensive varieties—French Colombard and Carignan—which were highly recommended in the fifties and sixties as big producers for generic white and generic red—jug wines.

Now the ideal is to make a wine that is not interchangeable with anyone else's. A wine that's immune to market conditions because it's so special. We seem to be headed toward a kind of melting pot or quiltwork wine, mixing grapes from different areas that find a common ground at T-T. We are undoubtedly inspired by the so-called Super Tuscan wines from Italy, which fetch $40 a bottle. Also, Sangiovese has roots in the pre-Prohibition era, when the Italian immigrants brought over vine cuttings to make house wines. And since we're not tied to any restrictions about what to plant, the potential seems endless.

Finding the source of the bud wood to plant Sangiovese wasn't easy. Very little is being propagated in California, and you can't just bring it in from Italy any more. It is illegal. As with any agricultural product, you would be opening your vineyard and your neighbors to potential bug and disease problems.

The first stop in looking for bud wood is FPMS, the Foundation Plant Material Service of the University of California at Davis. Davis and Fresno state are the two viticultural and enology schools in California. Davis has a repository for tested and certified clonal material, but Forrest was only able to buy enough Sangiovese to graft twenty vines. None of the grape nurseries he contacted had any. He had to find a grower who would sell us 3,000 cuttings. Only two growers were really large enough—Atlas Peak and Robert Pepi. Atlas Peak refused to sell us any for still undetermined reasons. Robert Pepi, south of Yountville in the Napa Valley, was the only source. Forrest tasted Pepi's 1988 Sangiovese in barrels, looked at the 1989 crop out on the vine and went on the gut feeling that it was going to work at T-T. To choose bud wood you have to first taste the grapes from the source as close to harvest as possible. Then wait a year until the cane starts to lignify. Fresh bud wood has to be cut off the vine when the cane starts to do this—turn from a green shoot to brown wood, usually in mid-August. Knowing how a new grape will then translate into a wine is an educated guess. It comes with tasting and having a dream. It requires memory, a taste for quality, and heightened sensitivity—like being able to discern the different instruments in a piece of music.

Bud wood costs ten cents a bud. It used to be free, or be available at just the cost of cutting it, but demand for hard-to-find varieties like Sangiovese and the hassle of doing it has driven up the price.

Every year, shortly before harvest, we taste through all of our back vintages of Cabernet to see how the wines are evolving. Forrest and I pulled them out of the library, which is just a tucked-away area in our disgorging cellar, with metal ware-house-type shelving stacked with cases and a tall rolling ladder so we can get up to the oldest vintages. At first we thought we'd pour all the wines at once—a massive tasting—twelve glasses each—but as soon as we uncorked the 1978, we realized we weren't going to evaluate these wines. We wanted to enjoy them. One of the reasons it takes such a long time to make good wine is that there are so many factors to weigh and each bottle delivers its share of memories.

VERTICAL TASTING

1978 Our first vintage with the Iron Horse label. We have about ten cases left. Drinking better than ever. Very concentrated blackberry, black-cherry fruit, tar, a little alcohol. Still a little astringent. Tannin still showing. Young, sweet, and firm. Evolving. Far from fading as it sits in the glass, it becomes herbaceous. Maybe this flavor characteristic is a precursor to the cigar-box quality so admired in older Cabernets. That green-leaf character as it becomes oxidized becomes smoky and burnt like tobacco leaf.

1978 was a very chaotic year at Iron Horse. If you read the label carefully, you'll notice it says "grown, cellared, and bottled by Iron Horse Vineyards." Forrest actually produced the wine at Sonoma Vineyards. Our winery was under construction. My parents converted their garage into a bonded warehouse to age the wine in barrels.

It was a good, warm vintage, remarkable compared to 1977, which was one of the least exciting vintages of the seventies. 1974 is still considered the best of the decade. Some experts contend that California's golden age for wine began in 1976 at a now-legendary comparative blind tasting in Paris. To its shock and everlasting dismay, a panel of French judges gave top place to a 1973 California Cabernet from Stag's Leap Wine Cellars, ahead of such prestigious châteaux as Mouton Rothschild and Haut-Brion. For good measure, a California Chardonnay from Napa's Château Montelena bested a comparably distinguished flight of white burgundies.

. . .

1979 Tastes very young. Much younger than the '78. It's gripping, lean, the nose is still intensely fruity. This is the first vintage Forrest made here at the winery. Still can't guess how the wine will turn out. It could be great or it might never soften. Today it is quite closed. Letting it breathe and swirling it in the glass releases the aromas. This was a good vintage for us. Hot spring, cool summer. Controversial because it was quite good to excellent in Sonoma, whereas, in Napa, not so good. We have only one case and some magnums remaining in inventory. This is Forrest's son's birth year. We have to be careful about drinking it until the year 2,000, when Michael turns twenty-one.

1980 This has never been one of Forrest's favorites. He feels he lost control of the fruit. When it was young and we were trying to sell it, Forrest thought it was overly fruity, almost like blackcherry cough syrup. He felt it was alcoholic but did have good acid. Often wines you didn't like come around and surprise you. In the case of this '80, the fruit has toned down from garish to pleasingly bright. The acid has held the wine together and the wine keeps changing in the glass, a sign of complexity. But Forrest is unforgiving. He thinks the wine is overpowering, plummy, and porty. One of the perplexing things about wine making is that if you blow a wine, you can't just start over. That's it for the year and it will continue to haunt you until every last bottle is consumed. Fortunately, we produce so many wines there are bound to be more successes than not. 1980 was an excellent vintage for Chardonnay, Pinot Noir, and it is our first vintage of sparkling wine. Laurence and Terry, my brother and sister-in-law, were married in December 1980. Our dwindling supply of Pinot Noir is their anniversary wine.

. . .

1981 Lots of briary fruit. A little astringency in the nose. Strong bouquet. Very bright. Cranberry with citrus, very pretty complexity. Missing something in the middle. 1981 was a cool year. This vintage prompted Forrest's thoughts about blending.

1982 Forrest automatically decants this vintage, because over the years of opening it he knows it has a lot of sediment, whereas '81 does not. The '81 is lighter and might not hold up to the oxidization that goes along with decanting. The 1982 is still so young it can use a little air. It has so much zing and elegance, and seems to be developing complexity without losing its freshness. This is a wine we drink quite often—whenever we have special guests—out of magnums. It's one of our favorite vintages. At the Sonoma County Wine Auction, a barrel of this wine was chosen by a panel of wine makers—our peers—as the best of show from the Alexander Valley. It's alive in your mouth. Firm, bold, rich, and maturing. Smoky and silky. It has cherry, chocolate, cedar, and lemon in the background.

The '82 is going through a phase when the acid sticks out a little bit in the finish like a twist over a cup of espresso. This is akin to the '81 in that both wines were acidulated. At the time, adding acid to lower the Ph in red wines was considered standard wine-making technique to help the wines live longer, but since 1985, this hasn't been necessary. The vineyards have matured, so the fruit is naturally better balanced and more often has the ability to stand on its own. One of the side effects of acidulation is that the wine is apt to throw more tartrate crystals, which look like tiny amethysts on the cork and the rim of the bottle.

1982 was our last vintage of Zinfandel. It was a lovely wine, but expendable. The decision to switch to Cabernet Franc has proved itself by the drop in California Zinfandel sales from 3 to 2 percent of the entire market.

In Bordeaux, 1982 was the vintage that put Robert Parker on the map. The attorney turned wine writer called '82 the vintage of the century. He gave Pétrus a perfect score, driving the Bordeaux market wild.

1983 A light version of the '82. This vintage was confirmation that Forrest was headed in the right direction with blending. 1983 was an El Niño year. Cold and wet. The vines didn't look good all through the growing season. There were lots of bugs and Forrest didn't know how or even want to deal with them. We were worried we had oak root fungus, which could have destroyed the vineyard. We had fungus attacks—early Botrytis, phomopsis, late Botrytis—and then rain. We consequently harvested fruit that was not fully mature and had to be very carefully hand sorted at great loss to protect the quality of what wine we did make. It really shook Forrest up. He was not pleased with the outcome of that vintage with any of our wines. The 1983 Chardonnay was extremely tight and austere. This is the first vintage of Chardonnay I was given to sell.

1984 Very ripe, warm, slightly burnt fruit—plums and prunes. It really fits the vintage, which was quite hot. There was a little shower before harvest and Father and Forrest were gun shy. They didn't want to suffer another vintage like '83, so Father campaigned very heavily to make more Blanc de Blancs, picking

Chardonnay at 20 degrees Brix sugar for sparkling instead of holding out to make still wine. (The Brix scale is a hydrometer scale used to measure the approximate sugar content of grape juice.) As it turned out, the weather became very warm—an Indian summer—producing the richest Chardonnay we had ever made. The Fumé was also good, not unusual in a warm year. Most important, we learned when to pick our fruit for Sparkling at full maturity.

After a time in the glass, the 1984 Cabernet tastes bright, fruity, and is quite "sweet" smelling. There is plenty of alcohol in the wine, which is probably why it was so warming initially and later gives off that sweet smell. Very often alcohol comes across as a perception of sweetness. Alcohol also gives weight to a wine. There is a juiciness in the finish that comes from good acidity. Forrest thinks the wine is "right there."

1985 Now here is a good bottle of wine. 1985 was an exceptional year. It was hyped by all the wine writers as California's vintage of the decade. This is a lucky wine for us, because it was our first blend in such an exceptional vintage. And it is just now beginning to show how harmoniously Cabernet Sauvignon and Cabernet Franc blend together. Neither sticks out in any way. They are perfectly integrated to produce a new flavor. This was a big energy year for Forrest. He made a commitment to making much better wines. I want to say it was me, but, truthfully, Forrest had taken up horseback riding. He won a silver buckle for the Tevis Ride, a 100-mile endurance race in twenty-four hours across the spine of the Sierras. That got him in shape. He became very athletic, which seemed to get his brain going.

Today, the '85 very much resembles a wine Forrest and I

tasted at lunch in December 1988 in Tuscany. Neither of us can remember the label. It was recommended by the sommelier when Forrest asked about Sangiovese wines

Initially, it tastes very cherry, "sweet," and alcoholic. A great drink. As it evolves in the glass, it is becoming tannic, astringent. It is a very big rich wine that gets rapidly younger as it is exposed to air. It just shows how mysterious and meandering red wines can be. Theoretically, air should make it mature, not close up. There must be some chemical reason why it is reacting this way.

1986 Denser than 1985. Higher percentage of Cabernet Franc. 32 percent. Also reflects a bit more knowledge about growing the variety. The 1986 is going through a "weedy" stage. Red wines age longer than white wines, but not necessarily in a set, linear way. White wines tend to intensify. Reds keep changing direction. Ours tend to be fruity and approachable when young, then after two years in the bottle harden up and go into this weedy stage. It can take up to a couple or more years to come out of that phase when the fruit returns to the fore.

This was an upswing vintage. We were riding a high from '85. The weather cooperated. We were in the groove. '86 is the first year we really started to use vatting—letting the wine sit on the skins for a couple of weeks, which makes it more supple. This wine got a 90 in *The Spectator*. We also made some breakthrough sparkling wines, like the 1986 LD and the Vrais Amis, which we will release this October.

With air, the Cabernets seem very meaty, juicy, with that perception of sweetness that's very reminiscent of Italian wines. This is an element Forrest wants to push in the wines. That's why we're planting Sangiovese.

With more time in the glass, the fruit volitizes, disappears, exposing the tannins and the alcohol. The wine is still unresolved. It's acting adolescent.

1987 A great vintage. Exceptional intensity and depth of character. This blend is 63 percent Cabernet Sauvignon and 37 percent Cabernet Franc. It is going to be a staggering wine once the edges soften and all the blocks of flavors start to flow together. This is the first truly exceptional vintage from T-T. The deep purple *"robe"*—*robe* is a French term that refers to a wine's color and appearance—intense cassis and sweet cedar nose are exactly what Forrest says he sensed when walking through the vineyards that summer. The wine has perfect fruit, lovely weight, and an endless finish. 1987 is the year Forrest and I decided to get together.

1988 Same blend as 1987 but not as intense. More approachable. A very tasty drink. Again, Cabernet Sauvignon in the bouquet, Cabernet Franc showing through in the mid-palate, and Cabernet Sauvignon in the finish. Due for release in October. It's just a kid.

1989 We came up with two blends that will be bottled separately. That'll confuse the marketplace!

1990 This wine will be blended and bottled in 1992, released in 1993.

Red wines are unpredictable. You can never be certain how they are going to show. Father has collected every great Bordeaux vintage since the 1920s and they all have gone through dumb stages. At one point he thought all of his '70's, a substantial amount of wine, had gone over the hill. Later they came back and are now drinking beautifully again. Wine is a living, breathing thing, and part of the fun is watching it change in the bottle. The true collector has to be philosophical. Every bottle is different, and can easily disappoint or thrill. Oxidization is essentially how wines age. Humidity, light, and temperature are also critical factors, hence the legendary stories of red wines buried in Scottish castles lost deep in the moors, with collections of good drinking Bordeaux from the 1860s and 1870s locked like a time capsule in collapsed cellars or vaults: 45 degrees, 100 percent humidity, and no light. We have a bottle given to us by our friend George Smith, which came out of just such a collection. It had been suspended in time at 43°F. As in art and antiques, provenance is very important in collecting wine.

One of the biggest wine scandals just now unfolding hinges on the question of provenance. It has to do with a secret cache of 1736 Château Lafite, which allegedly belonged to Thomas Jefferson. A German collector and wine merchant, Hardy Rodenstock, says he found it in a Parisian cellar. Malcolm Forbes bought one of the bottles at auction for $150,000 in 1985. A New York retailer had another, which shattered when he dropped it at a tasting. Now, a third is being challenged as a fraud. It was uncorked at a German wine institute, with the highly respected Christie's wine auctioneer Michael Broadbent officiating. After a year-long series of tests, the institute disclosed that 60 percent of the wine was from 1962. Mr. Rodenstock says he has one bottle left that he is willing to have tested but he refuses to disclose his source. All of the Jefferson labels reputedly have the initials Th.J., the vintage and Lafite misspelled with two *t*'s, presumably following the English use of double consonants, as in the Declaration of Independence.

Jefferson was an avid collector. He was the unofficial wine advisor for the first three administrations in the White House, including his own. He also kept a large cellar at Monticello, ordered his wines directly from the châteaux and even grew grapes to make wine in Virginia. Lafite routinely tops off and recorks its wines for vintages of comparable quality. 1962 is a good year, but an almost two-thirds "top off" makes one question whether you and Jefferson are having the same wine experience.

Aging generally intensifies the natural aromas of the wine into new and different smells abstractly called "bottle bouquet." The alcohol doesn't change. The acidity doesn't change. The Ph doesn't change. The structure of the wine doesn't change. Bouquet, color, flavors, and tannins are like the face of a wine. They change over time and, hopefully, become more interesting.

How long a wine ages depends on intensity of fruit, higher alcohol, higher degree of acidity, lack of bacterial contamination, and, in the case of reds, intensity of color—no brown. A black-purple Cabernet will age longer than a garnet-brown Merlot. Color varies from grape to grape. One of the reasons why Cabernet Sauvignon, in particular, ages so well is its dark red to purplish hue. As the wine ages, it goes through stages of bright-red brick to brown. Usually a very dark wine is more tannic than a light wine. But tannins alone do not allow a wine to age. Excessive tannin will never soften. A classic example is 1945 Château Pétrus, which still hasn't softened to this day. Acid is an important element in holding a wine together along with tannin, alcohol, color, and flavor. One of the great wine debates is whether a wine that tastes delicious when young will be able to withstand the test of time.

An older wine needs to sit upright and then be decanted to pour off the clear wine. Undecanted, the wine is murky. If the sediment is chunky it will settle very quickly. If it's very fine, it might take months. The amount of sediment that falls out of suspension to the bottom of the bottle is exactly the same as the sediment that originally went into the bottle with the wine— dead yeast cells, bits of wood, and particles of dirt.

Any opinion about the best time to drink a wine is purely subjective. The English like their wines aged longer, which is something akin to liking your meat well done. It's their tradition to drink a weightier style. Cold nights around the fire with a joint of beef just call for it.

Part of the excitement of drinking older wines is the history attached to them. It's a really special gift to search out the most age-worthy wine of a vintage for a newborn to enjoy twenty-one years later. 1929, for example, was a legendary vintage in Bordeaux, the year the stock market collapsed, and when Father was born. Today, 1929 Lafite costs $8,000 to $10,000 a bottle.

Father's cellar is dwindling as we happily drink it up. As he gets older, he buys mostly wines that are ready to drink. One of his greatest pleasures is visiting his favorite Armagnac producer. It takes a whole afternoon of tasting before Father talks the man into parting with some of his fifty year old. Then the two of them, three sheets to the wind, syphon some out of the barrel and hand label the bottles themselves.

Father used to say he was born wearing a tie and grew up wanting to be a lawyer. He started Stanford when he was sixteen and passed the Bar before graduating from law school in the same class with Supreme Court Justices William Rhenquist and Sandra Day O'Connor. Grandpa Dave would walk around the country club bragging that his sons worked day and night, to which Father would complain, "Daddy, please don't say that. If your sons were smarter, they wouldn't have to work night and day." Father is a very passionate and vigorous man. At some point, he just became weary of the law. And he was tired of dealing in something so ephemeral as advice, heeded or not. Both my parents wanted a tangible product of their own creating that would have lasting value and that could be evaluated. He says the only way he'll go back full time to practicing law is if the client tells him something he hasn't heard before.

My parents first went to Europe for Father's thirtieth birthday. It was one of those whirlwind, "If this is Belgium, it must be Tuesday" kind of trips—eight cities in twelve days. That is when he decided to live in France. He became a Conseil Juridique five years later, and practiced international law. Right after we moved from Los Angeles to Paris, my parents started looking for a wine estate. For Father's thirty-eighth birthday, Mother gave him an IOU for a tractor, once they found the right property. Father considered a place in Armagnac but passed after he figured out that after planting a crop, plus a minimum of twenty years in the cask he would be sixty-seven by the time he could really enjoy his first vintage.

Sheer fate brought them home to California—a combination of business and family matters. Mother first heard about Iron Horse at a Beverly Hills dinner party. It took longer to negotiate the factory-direct Lamborghini tractor than it did to buy the property. As Mother said, the dream became the reality and the reality became the folly. Initially, Father was the cash crop. For years he commuted to Los Angeles to lawyer four days a week, while Mother ran Iron Horse and Forrest was part-time vineyard manager. All kinds of consultants were brought in, but their best advice came from an old-time Sonoma grape-grower who said, "Barry, listen to all the consultants you want, but in the end the decisions are yours. You don't have to be an expert on anything but your own property and you'll come to learn it better than anyone else."

Father now thinks of us as landed gentry. One day he was enjoying the shade of his garden after lunch, lying on a chaise longue with his loyal dog, Max, at his feet. He was wearing a Sea Island cotton shirt with a discreet "B" monogrammed on the pocket, beige pants, his silver Iron Horse belt, and cowboy boots. I said, "Daddy, you look like a Ralph Lauren ad." I meant it as a compliment, but he was miffed. "Ralph Lauren is just an imitation of people like us," he said.

Harvest and Winemaking

SEPTEMBER

LABOR DAY was the official start of summer in San Francisco. It was ninety degrees, and we finally began getting ready for harvest. It's been a long time coming and we've had no choice but to be stoic.

Harvest is the culmination of the growing season. It's a three-ring circus, with the grapes coming in, fermentation underway, and we are entertaining every day for harvest lunch. Unfortunately, the fall selling season coincides with harvest. The major trade tastings are usually clumped together in September and October.

Forrest is very fastidious about how he wants the winery to look to receive the grapes. Everything gets a good cleaning. There won't be another chance once harvesting starts. We touch up the paint, test the conveyers, the crushers, the presses, and the pumps, which have been idle for ten months. And we prepare the barrels.

You have to stick your head in every barrel, smell it, and inspect it with a high-intensity light. Used barrels can smell like vinegar when they are dry, or there can be mold. We roll the barrels outside in front of the winery, wash them out with a cleaning solution and then rinse them with warm water and citric acid.

New barrels arrive in a container from France. We coat the outside with a mildicide to prevent mold, protect against scraping and also to deter barrel borers, tiny insects like termites, which have a particularly keen appetite for French oak. Then the new barrels are numbered so we can keep track of them. All the barrels—old plus new, amounting to about 800—are soaked up, which means filling them with water to swell the wood to tighten the staves and make sure the barrels are leak-free for the vintage.

The lifespan of a barrel is five years. The new ones—we buy 100 to 200 a year—are used the first year to ferment white wine. We buy a combination of tight-grained oaks from the forests of Nevers, Alier, and Vosges in central and northern France. We order them to be toasted or charred over a hot fire to our specifications as they are being assembled by the cooper.

Each cooper has a particular style, which results in distinct flavors in the finished wine. The secret is to learn which style best suits your wine. The best coopers command the highest prices and you always get what you pay for. Top-quality barrels cost $600 apiece.

New oak imparts very dominant flavors. You have to match it carefully with the fruit and the style of wine you are making. Two- to three-year-old oak barrels tend to let more of the fruit flavors come to the fore. After three years, the inside of the barrels are shaved and retoasted so they can be used another two seasons for red wine. We use some new barrels for red wine, but because red wine stays in the barrel for eighteen months to two years, the wine will pick up more oak flavors and an overdose would kill the fruit. Once barrels have been used for red wine, they can never go back to white wine. After the barrel's prime, it drops in value to about $20, at which point we just cut them in half and use them as planters.

· · ·

According to ancient lore, grapes ripen with the waxing of the moon, which would put harvest at mid-month. The weather is cooperating. It seems as if we are going to luck out, and the dire predictions were unwarranted. This close to maturity, the Pinot Noir clusters, usually the first to be harvested, have turned completely, from green to purple. The Sauvignon Blanc is softening and becoming translucent. Cabernet and Chardonnay are still a ways off, but the flavors of all the varieties are developing day by day.

September 14. First day of harvest. It is a wine-making decision where and when to pick. This is the time that, when you taste the juice from a berry, you can in fact taste the wine. You can taste the intensity and the length. You taste the grapes, not only for sweetness, but for their balance and the lingering flavor. If you can actually taste the flavor of the grape for four, five, ten seconds after you put it into your mouth, the wine made from those grapes is going to have the same degree of intensity. The essence of harvest is to pick the grapes when they have reached the optimum of flavor maturity, not necessarily chemical maturity as it would be defined by Brix, acid, or Ph measurements. You have to understand what the flavor character is for each section of the vineyard that you farm. You actually develop a track record and a palate memory, so that when you wander through a vineyard and taste the berries, you compare them much as you do individual vintages of wine. What to pick and where is up to Forrest, and he tells Manuel. Manuel's talent is how to coordinate crews so they cover the whole vineyard without overlapping or neglecting any rows; and, also because of the terrain, you want to deploy the crews so they have lighter loads on the way up the hills.

"The idea," says Forrest, "is to achieve a wine that tastes like what I taste in the vineyard when the grapes are at their height of maturity. Once we get the fruit into the winery the idea is to just not screw it up."

At 6:30 A.M., Forrest went up to the equipment yard where the pickers had congregated. Manuel was taking the roll, writing down Social Security numbers, and assigning picking crews. There were some new faces, but most of the guys come back year after year.

We pick up between twelve and sixteen additional workers for harvest. Migrant workers start coming up to the winery looking for work in late August, just as the local apple harvest is waning. Having our harvest so late this year has kept many of them out of work for almost a month. Fortunately, it looks like they will be rewarded with a good crop in '91—easy to pick and bountiful. Pickers are paid by the bin. They were very badly hurt in short years like '88 and '90, but this harvest a fast worker could easily make $14 an hour.

Once the full crew is assembled, Forrest speaks to the men in Spanish. He explains the work rules, safety rules, and our bonus system for quality. He holds up two bunches of grapes "this is mature fruit," he says, "and this is not. This is bonus fruit and this is not." Each picker comes equipped with his own knife. If he doesn't, we'll supply him one at cost. A picking knife is about six inches long and it has a curved, serrated, stainless-steel blade. Each picker has a particular way he likes his knife—either with a string attached to the handle so it dangles on his wrist between cuts, or tape around the handle to make it more comfortable. It needs to be very sharp to cut through the stems. The best picker will harvest fifty lugs a day. Each lug holds thirty-five pounds. About 7,000 clusters.

It is exciting when the first grapes are brought to the winery. Everybody wants to have a look and taste. It takes about two hours for a full press load to be assembled. We all just stand around—not quite sure whether we should go back to our offices or wait for the next ceremony.

Every winery has some sort of ceremony commemorating the beginning of harvest. Robert Mondavi invites the bishop to come and bless the grapes. We usually toast with sparkling wine, but this year we brought in Sauvignon Blanc before Pinot Noir for sparkling, so we had to quickly change our toasting wine and glassware. Obviously, you can't fall into any routines with farming. We sort of muddled through a modified version of pouring our 1990 Fumé Blanc over the first press load with our nondenominational blessing: "Here's to a great harvest, cheers!"

From here on out, the winery crew really shines. There's so much to do and the pace is fast. There's a certain misconception among city dwellers that country living is nice and easy. That's actually rather true during much of the year, but not during harvest. We don't walk about our business, we run. The men picking in the field get paid by the box. They get into a rhythm that sends them flying down the rows. You can see the tops of the vines shaking while the men are hacking off the clusters. Then they run to load the bins onto the back of the tractor. The bins get tied down with bicycle straps. It's not easy getting up and down our hills, and the bins tip over easily. The first day we brought in twenty tons.

Once harvest is in full swing, we fall into a routine of waking up early, checking the sky, checking the barometer, and checking the weather channel. Forrest goes up to the winery for a quick look at 7:00 A.M. It is just beginning to have that wonderful smell of fermenting wine—sweet fruit with a tinge of carbon dioxide that pricks your nose. Because it is cool and the doors have been shut, the smells accumulate in the winery overnight. The floors are damp from being hosed down. And it is quiet. The men are in the fields. Forrest ducks into the lab, where two interns, usually U.C. Davis students, are measuring the temperature, sugar, Ph, and acidity of the juice in all of the tanks. Then they rack the juice that was pressed just the day before and allowed to settle overnight in a chilled tank. The clear juice gets pulled off and is pumped to a clean tank. The lees or solids—the pips and the dirt that sifted to the bottom of the tank—are filtered and recombined with the juice. The leftover cake of heavy sediment is composted and put back into the vineyard. We add yeast to the tank to induce fermentation.

Each wine requires a specialized strain of yeast. For sparkling wine, we use a bayanus strain, which we get from Champagne. The selection of yeast is purely subjective. There is a perpetual debate about the ideal yeast for each wine. The result is that, with modern freeze-dry technology, we are able to experiment with specialized yeast strains isolated from all the great wine-producing regions of the world. For sparkling wine, you want the first fermentation to be very clean, not overly agitated, and to start up within two days. It should take off slowly at about 20 degrees Brix sugar, and accelerate as the yeast cells multiply. It should then slow down again as the sugar decreases and the alcohol increases—a bell-shaped curve that lasts about ten days to two weeks. For our Cabernets, we want a very vigorous fermentation that can keep going at a higher alcohol level and that tends to extract more color and flavor from the skins. By about 8:00 A.M., Forrest heads out into the vineyards with Manuel to check how harvest is going, if everyone in the crew has shown up, and to say good morning to the harvesters and tractor drivers. He walks down the rows, tasting the grapes, mentally comparing this harvest to years past for flavor and yield. If he feels too much mature fruit is being left on the vine, or fruit is being dropped on the ground, or if the workers are gathering too many leaves, Forrest will advise the tractor drivers and reinforce their responsibility to oversee the picking crews. The drivers get paid by the hour, plus a bonus according to the picking quality of their respective crews.

September 25. The first grapes of the day come into the winery between 8:00 and 9:00 A.M. The harvest boxes are stacked on a pallet in the field and brought in by tractor no more than an hour after the grapes have been picked. The pallets get weighed on a portable electronic scale. Shirley is in charge. She sets up a card table, a chair with a cushion on it, her record books, and a calculator. Forrest, Raphael, John, and my father look over her shoulder throughout the day, trying to calculate a load for the press, figuring the yield per acre, and how much wine we will make. The press holds 4.5 metric tons of grapes and we want to keep each block of the vineyard separate. Coordinating the harvesting with the maturity of the fruit, running the presses at capacity, having the tanks available to keep the juice separate, and setting a pace so the picked grapes do not sit out in the sun, is like playing with a Rubik's Cube.

The yields per acre vary from vintage to vintage. Every day

as the grapes come in we rewrite our sale projections. We have to keep an open mind. How the harvest goes in terms of quality and quantity determines how much Chardonnay and Pinot Noir we will make versus sparkling. Most of the vineyard is fairly clearly delineated as to which grapes are best for still or sparkling wine. As the new vineyards come into production, the balance is changing in favor of sparkling wine. But Forrest might still look at a particular block—say in a dry year, if the vines are stressed or stalled at 20 degree Brix sugar, which would be perfect for sparkling, but nowhere near maturity for Chardonnay. Conversely, there may be a block traditionally picked for sparkling which by some quirk begs to be left on the vine for a few more weeks for still wine.

Forrest makes a gut decision on what will make the best wine. Business considerations also come into play. We have invested in barrels and equipment and a staff for a projected amount of wine. And we like to keep a certain market position by maintaining a degree of continuity—as much as we can, since we are an estate-bottled winery. From the very beginning, Forrest and my parents decided we would not buy grapes and even the painfully lean vintages have not changed our minds.

The grapes for sparkling are stacked in boxes on pallets in front of the winery, attracting thousands of bees. Everyone on the winemaking staff gets stung at least once a year. We all pick at the grapes as we walk back and forth. The concentration of flavors and the texture of the skins give us an inkling of what the wine will taste like.

The pallets are forklifted through the front doors of the winery and down the main aisle that is lined with steel tanks on either side to a conveyor belt. A bucket brigade of all the winery personnel load the grapes onto the conveyor as gently as possible so they do not bruise or rupture. The first boxes are put on the concrete pad alongside the conveyor to catch any grapes that fall off the sides. And two people—Raphael and either Forrest or my father—sort through the grapes as they go into the press, discarding leaves and underripe fruit or any clusters with rot. This is where they can check each picker's work to determine who will receive bonuses for quality at the end of the day. After the first press load, Forrest can usually tell who is doing a good job and who is not and soon he will go back out into the vineyard to reinspire the men.

It takes about thirty minutes to load the press—ten tons of whole grape clusters falling loosely into a stainless steel cylinder that is highly polished and designed by a French firm in Champagne to give the most delicate juice possible. Inside the press is a white, Teflon-coated membrane that looks like a boat canvas and is about an eighth of an inch thick. When it is inflated slightly, it gently pushes the grapes together and juice flows through slotted screens out of the bottom of the press.

The press cycle lasts from one and a half to two hours and yields 140 gallons per ton, which is then separated into two parts: free-run juice and press lots. The first ten gallons go into the press tank because the first gush of juice out of the press is murky. The last twenty-five gallons are the most extracted. The free run in between is the cleanest, most delicate, and most flavorful. It is the best grape juice you will ever taste, though you should not drink too much of it. One glass is like two bunches of grapes.

The Chardonnay for sparkling is almost green, not quite clear and slightly frothy as it gushes out of the press. It smells like green apples and spice and it tastes something like apples with citrus, both sweet and tart. The Pinot Noir comes out a pale salmon color. It smells like berries and cherries with a wonderful tang in the finish. It is difficult to taste many nuances at this point. You are looking for balance and a long finish. The intensity of the fruit you taste now should always be there throughout the whole wine-making process unless bad wine making strips it of flavor.

The juice is pumped into a refrigerated tank and left to settle. The pumice—spent skins and seeds—is dumped into the back of a flatbed truck. It is astonishing how much juice flows down the sides of the truck onto the gravel—probably thirty gallons a ton. This is useless to us, because if we pressed any harder we would extract too much harshness and bitterness from the skins. For sparkling wine, you are trying to get the juice from the heart of the grape between the skin and the seeds, and if you walk over to the truck and pick up a fistful of pumice, you will see that the action of the press is so gentle that the skins of any slightly hard, immature grapes are not even broken. Now the press is cleaned out and ready for another load. If the weather is cool and the picking is going well, we can do four press loads a day.

Raphael is at the press watching the juice flow out. "Are you happy?" "Yes," he says. "The juice looks good and smells good." Forrest is also pleased by how smoothly harvest is running. No glitches. I mention this to John and he crosses his fingers. "Let's just hope it stays this way." Shirley is ecstatic about the size of the crop. So far, we're up 20 percent. Laurence figures we should make about 7,000 cases of Chardonnay. That would mean 22,000 cases of sparkling. Forrest and I agree that this ratio fits the image of the winery. Besides, the 1990 Chardonnay is going to be so successful. It will set up the 1991 nicely. Forrest takes me out in the vineyard. He wants the crews to stop for today. Block L is next, but he'd rather hold off until tomorrow morning so the grapes will be "right there." It takes two to two-and-a-half weeks to harvest all of the grapes for sparkling. It depends on how the individual blocks ripen. Some days you have to stop to wait for the fruit to mature. It is hard to say "We are not picking today." The crew is so wound up they do not want to quit.

During our years of wine making, just about every conceivable disaster has occurred including a tractor blowing up and power failures in the winery, which become critical if they last for more than a day because we lose all our refrigeration. We even survived having our state-of-the-art, very sensitive German wine press die on us with a full load of grapes one Sunday afternoon. We had to Rube Goldberg it back together ourselves.

September 30. The Sauvignon Blanc from Forrest's property usually overlaps with the sparkling. We have a second press and sufficient tanks and barrels to handle it. We pull two tractors and two crews from Iron Horse and send them to T-T. The grapes get trucked back to the winery. Sauvignon Blanc is easy to harvest because of the way it hangs on the vine. It is very exposed. The pickers love it. They can fly right through it, but because it gets very warm at T-T, we only want to pick from 7 to 10 in the morning, which limits the crews to only ten to twelve tons a day.

The first load usually arrives at the winery around lunchtime. Forrest is always especially proud to see the fruit arrive from his vineyard, and Victor, his foreman, knows exactly how Forrest wants it presented—perfectly mature fruit and no leaves, prompting *oohs* and *ahs* as we all look over the bins. The grapes are fat and round and usually a honeydew-melon green. Forrest hedges the vines to let more sunlight through to the grapes, which turns the skins a honey color when they are ripe. The natural grassy tendency of Sauvignon Blanc seems to be concentrated in the skins. The heart of the grape tastes like melons, figs, pineapple, papaya, and peach—very exotic, and if you suck on the skins of the grapes, it is like chewing on a blade of grass. The more golden-colored grapes tend to have less of that grassiness and a much more floral, perfumelike quality.

Forrest also keeps the crop small. Sauvignon Blanc is a very heavy producing variety. It can comfortably produce, on good soils, up to eight tons to the acre. The average yield throughout the North Coast is five to six tons to the acre, Forrest's vineyard averages about four. His theory is that if the vines are not working all that hard, they will set more flavor in the berries. Also, growing a smaller crop means there is little need for supplemental irrigation, even on the marginal soils at T-T. The added water would merely plump up the berries and take away from the intensity of flavor.

The crews load the Sauvignon Blanc in 1000-pound gondolas, steel bins that stack easily on the back of a flatbed truck for the thirty-mile drive over country roads to Iron Horse. The most critical factor in hauling the grapes is not to macerate the fruit before it gets to the winery. If the fruit gets mashed, the juice will oxidize in the gondola and could set off a spontaneous fermentation. As soon as the grapes arrive at the winery, the bins are unloaded by forklift, weighed, and taken over to the stemmer-crusher—an ingenious machine that pulls the grapes off the stems. The forklift raises the bin twelve feet off the ground, empties it into a stainless-steel hopper with a six-inch auger at the bottom that moves the grapes into a cylinder with a slow-turning, slotted screen on the outside and paddles on the inside, which turn at very high revolutions. The paddles knock the grapes off the stems and push them through the slotted screen and into another hopper. The stems are about four to five inches long, too long to get through the slots. The centrifugal force of the paddles drives them out the end of the machine, where they pile up in a heap.

The crushed grapes are pumped through a rather clumsy-looking piston pump that chunks away as the juice is pumped into stainless-steel pipes that wrap around the upper inside wall of the winery and then out the back to the presses. Half go directly into the press and the other into overhead holding tanks positioned high above the presses, in contact with the skins and the seeds so that they pick up more flavor for six to eight hours. We come back to the winery at midnight. By then, the seeds and skins have settled to the bottom of the holding tank, and the juice has risen to the top, so we first can draw off the free-run juice relatively cleanly and then open a big valve gate at the bottom of the tank to let the pumice fall into the press.

When Forrest is playing ringmaster for all the action during harvest, he often does not get to stand at the press and be a wine maker. It is a special occasion when he and I go up to the winery together. We bring a thermos of coffee, a bottle of brandy, turn on the radio and with an intern and one of our permanent employees, Pony, press fifteen to sixteen tons of Sauvignon Blanc by the light of the moon. Pony usually gets night duty because he has a car that is reliable and he does not seem to mind getting up in the middle of the night.

Forrest hooks up a hose to a valve on the outside of the holding tanks, opens the valve, and the juice flows down into a stainless steel cart. I hold the hose. The juice that comes out is this fabulous green-gold color and it smells like freshly mown hay. It is wonderful to taste a glassful taken straight from the hose. It flows at a good rate for nearly half an hour, then it starts to peter out. When it stops, Forrest shuts off the valve and lowers the snout of the holding tanks directly into the press to release the remaining pumice. Despite the high-tech design, we end up wrapping plastic bags around it so the must—the lees—does not go flying. The bottom of the holding tanks have 18-inch gate valves that are pneumatically driven. If you open the valve too fast, it will flood the whole area. When Forrest opens the valves, there is this *whoosh!* and you can see the pumice start to flow out of the tank. These tanks are about thirty feet high. There is a very strong force of gravity, and you can fill the press with fifteen tons of crushed grapes in twenty seconds. The guys kneeling on top of the press, holding down the snout and the garbage bags around it, have to judge when the press is full and tell Forrest when to shut the valve. If it sticks or you do not close it fast enough, you could flood the whole platform with a sticky mess of grapes.

Losing five gallons of juice is not the end of the world, but hundreds of gallons could get wasted if you are not careful. Is the compressor running properly? Is air getting to the cylinders? Are all the valves hooked up properly? Is the pump hooked up correctly? Is the press locked into position? Is the top of the draining tank open? If it is not, the opened 18-inch valve at the bottom of the tank would suck in the sides of the stainless steel tank, and could end up looking like a crumpled beer can.

Once the press is loaded, Forrest sets the controls. Even though it is an automatic, he prefers to run it manually so he can constantly check the quality of the juice. Forrest presses his

Sauvignon Blanc to 130 gallons of free-run juice and twenty-five gallons of press juice.

The pressing cycle takes from one to two hours, depending on how slowly he wants to go, how many times he opens the press to look inside to see how dry the fruit is. You have to look at it. You cannot just push a button. You have to stop, climb up there, feel it, smell it, taste the juice as you press harder, then make a subjective decision as to when it is ready. Meanwhile, we chat, drink coffee and brandy, and dance to some bluesy, sexy love songs on the radio.

Those numbers—130 gallons of free run and twenty-five gallons of pressed juice—are very conservative. Traditionally, Sauvignon Blanc is pressed to 170–180 gallons per ton. We throw away 25–30 gallons of juice, but we know from experience the extra 25–30 gallons of juice of Sauvignon Blanc detract from the overall quality of our wine. Technology is at the point where now you can get every last little drop out of the grape. In the old days, when the ancient little guy was stomping it with his feet, he was getting 130 gallons a ton at most, maybe 125, and he was beating his brains out; we jumped from that to the technology of having a press that could extract over 200 gallons a ton. By the end of the press cycle the grapes were ground down as dry as sawdust. Just as you can use technology to improve quantity, what is exciting about winemaking today is using it to get the most delicate juice possible.

When Forrest decides that the grapes have been properly pressed, we pull up the truck alongside the press and dump the pumice—the spent grapes—into the truck to be composted the next morning. We clean out the press, make a few small checks, the sulphur dioxide (SO_2), the acidity, and the Ph, leave some notes for the morning crew, and go home.

· · ·

Thank goodness, Iron Horse doesn't depend on making Pinot Noir. Forrest didn't make any in 1981 or 1984. He bottled the 1989 as a Tin Pony wine and in 1990 he made so little—only 100 gallons, about forty cases worth—that it was not enough to fill the press. We crushed the grapes by hand.

There is one shy bearing knoll—the top of block G—behind the winery that Forrest used for a great string of Pinot Noirs in 1985, 1986, 1987, and 1988. He got about two and one half tons an acre off that knoll, which translate into 800 or so cases a year. He liked the knoll for still wine as opposed to sparkling because the grapes are smaller, more concentrated, and the skins are thicker, more tannic. The knoll is composed of very rocky shale and is relatively steep, so that drainage is good. It has easterly exposure—little afternoon sun—so a longer growing season. And the nights are cool. In warm climates, Pinot Noir results in thin-skinned grapes and bland-tasting wines.

Pinot Noir is the most difficult grape to grow. It is the most site-specific of all the grape varieties. Whether the grapes are from the top of the knoll or the bottom makes a big difference, and you never know what you are going to get. One year it will produce a very good crop and the next year nothing.

Now Forrest has transferred all his affection to a new knoll— two acres on the next hill over, which Forrest planted in 1986 as one big Pinot Noir experiment with two different clones—a Pommard clone from David Adelsheim's vineyard in Oregon and a Giesenheim clone that we call clone N from the research center in Germany. The knoll is called Laurence's knoll because, some years back, Laurence and I were standing behind the winery looking across the property when Laurence mused,

"You know, I can see my house on top of that knoll." He didn't move fast enough and now it's covered in vines. Forrest hopes to get his first commercial-size crop off Laurence's knoll in 1992. Mother has warned him that if he doesn't make any in '92 she'll make it herself. "And don't think I don't know how," she said, shaking her finger. Pinot Noir is her baby.

Iron Horse is becoming famous for our harvest lunches. This is Mother's job. During crush, she entertains 30 to 40 people a day, five days a week for six or seven weeks. Mark spends all day preparing the one meal.

As usual, all of the produce comes out of our gardens. As soon as one lunch is over, Mark writes the next day's menu so he can leave a picking list for Father. Father likes to pick early in the morning when it's cool.

> *Thursday Picklist*
> 6 bunches Italian parsley
> 1 bin assorted squash
> ½ bin assorted tomatoes
> ½ bin potatoes
> 1 bin of assorted chicories
> 1 basket of grapes
> 1 bin of pears

Mark complains that if he asks Father for twenty-five tomatoes he gets twenty-five *bins* of tomatoes. One bin is thirty pounds. For emphasis, Mother says, "That's your father. Try asking him for one rose."

Father doesn't trust any of us to pick vegetables. I asked him to stand in for me at two events in Los Angeles once, and rather than stay down there for the weekend, he flew back early Sunday morning and then returned to Los Angeles on Monday. "I don't think you appreciate the effort your mother and I put into these lunches," he said. "If I wasn't here, nobody would get fed."

Lunch is a groaning board under a wood-slat gazebo covered with roses and views of the harvest going on around us. There are platters of sliced tomatoes—a tasting feast of all the different varieties—white corn, and cold sliced potatoes drizzled with our own olive oil. All the meat and fish are local. Mark buys directly from the farmers or at the County Fair. Every day the menu changes. Mark never repeats himself during the entire period. The bottles of wine are just plunked down the middle of the picnic tables. Everything we produce is available to taste, and the luxury of it is that you don't have to finish anything. If you run out of wine glasses, you just dump what's left of one wine on the ground and switch to whatever else you want.

At some point during the meal, Father introduces each of us in the family. Everyday there's a new crowd. He tries to come up with something different to say to entertain us, but once he has globbed onto a good joke, he sticks with it. One of the interns, Brad Rubin, who worked the harvest with us this year, kept hearing how he was expected to go home to Massachusetts where his family distributes our wines "to get the numbers up." Since he's been home he has had a special Iron Horse quota to sell.

Mother does everything from wipe off the benches in the morning to seating the guests and getting them to mingle. She makes couples split up so conversation will be more interesting and also to give people something to talk about on their way home. After lunch, she welcomes everyone into her home for coffee. She and Mark get two days off per week, Tuesday and

Wednesday, but she says they aren't really days off because it's the only time we give her to get the house cleaned.

This year we will entertain 1,500 people at harvest lunch. Mother gets asked surprisingly often how she stands it. "Don't you get tired of people every day?" I wonder what they expect her to say. But she is always gracious, smiles, and says, "It's my pleasure." Anyone who appreciates the art of entertaining can't help being impressed. My parents are absolute masters at making everyone feel like an honored guest. You never know who you're going to meet at harvest lunch. The invitations go out to six thousand friends and customers around the world. You could as easily find yourself talking to a U.S. senator as a food-and-beverage director from Singapore. The only common denominator is Iron Horse. One day we had twenty absurdly young diplomats from Eastern Europe—in fact, they looked so young that when they were signing the guest book, Mother asked, "Are you all over twenty-one?" I started talking to one young blond I assumed was still a student. She corrected me, saying she worked for her country's embassy in Moscow—in charge of the political sector for Latvia. What do I know? I just sell wine.

My parents' home is like a small museum. There is so much to see. Almost forty years' worth of collecting art and antiques. Every nook and cranny is filled. There are flowers everywhere. Just going up the steps to the front door is the most fragrant experience, and then you walk through the house—through the living room and the dining room—out to the magical garden, where coffee is served under the cool, refreshing shade of the tall trees.

The house was built in 1876—a great old Victorian, which

was listing on a foundation of rusty beer cans when my parents first saw it. They completely restored it—repairing a big, wrap-around veranda and replacing the broken parts of the carpenter-Gothic gingerbread. Redwood boards were taken from a broken-down barn on the property and used for the paneling in the library and a full wall of bookshelves. They ran out of boards to cover all the beams, so Forrest gave them the wood from a chicken coop of the same vintage from his property. The plaster ceiling in the dining room was torn down, uncovering tongue-and-groove redwood that Mother loved and decided to keep bare. She found a roll of appliqué—which had come around the Horn but had never been used—of grapes hanging on the vine to encircle the ceiling. And friends from England found discontinued William Morris wallpapers that were rerun especially for her. Mother wanted and got the house done in nine months. She said that if you can have a baby in nine months, a house shouldn't take any longer.

OCTOBER

October 5. We have been sailing through the harvest. We are lucky we produce sparkling wine. It gives us an edge, because we harvest earlier for sparkling than for still wine. Not everybody is doing so well. We've already picked 350 tons of grapes—about half our total production—while many Cabernet growers are just beginning. Uncertainty about the weather keeps mounting. The days are getting shorter, leaves are turning color and falling off the trees. It's not unheard of to have October frost, let alone rain. The leaves on the vines are starting to yellow along the bottom of the canopy. These were the first leaves on the vine to come out, so they are the first to die. As long as it's green on the tops of the vines, they are still photosynthesizing, ripening the grapes. When all the leaves turn color, it means the vines have stopped growing, the grapes will not mature any further. It's autumn. You can smell it in the air. The light is softer. And it's dry—you kick up dust just walking through the vineyards. The soil feels like sand as it drifts through our fingers. The wild grasses are all burnt out. California gold, we call it, though a visitor might look at the color of the hills and say brown.

The winery crew is starting to look frayed. There are no days off during harvest. Raphael's back is out and he caught a cold; he's chain-smoking. There isn't an inch of shade where he stands to monitor the press, but he won't budge, so we set up an Italian market umbrella.

Plus, there's the double whammy of the market place. It's unnerving. Everyone is cutting down inventory, restaurants are closing, hotels are running at 40 percent occupancy. Consumption is just plain down. Anything that "doesn't move" gets struck from wine lists and there's still plenty of 1989 Chardonnay out there. September–October is when we switch vintages. Some wineries are beginning to deal by cutting special prices or giving away free goods. Even with a gorgeous wine like our '90, it's missionary work to get anybody excited. At least we've moved into the '90, and our prices are holding.

We started picking Chardonnay for still wine on October 7—two weeks later than last year. We've been testing the grapes since early September. First weekly, then daily. We cull a random sampling—a cluster from every tenth vine, every other row, one from the outside, one from the inside, one from the cane, one from the head, one from the western exposure, one from the eastern exposure. We crush the clusters into a bucket and take a sugar reading in the field with a refractometer—an instrument that looks like a flashlight with a prism on the end. There's a scale inside, and you have to look up into the light to get a measurement. The scale goes from zero to 32. Each degree of Brix is equivalent to approximately .60 degrees of alcohol. We harvest Chardonnay for still wine at 22.5 to 23 degree Brix sugar. The sugar converts to alcohol, which gives the wine weight, glycerin, "legs," but flavor is what separates the good vintages from the great. Deciding when to harvest is just like the old Gallo television commercial back in the seventies that showed a gray-haired wine maker tasting the grapes and nodding while the young enologist fiddled with his instrument.

Andrew says that when he's gathering samples at T-T, the foreman's yellow Labrador, Duffy, tags along. The dog can just reach up to eat the grapes. He knows to sample from various exposures and wags his tail when they're ready.

Some years, the grapes ripen through dehydration, which concentrates flavors. This year, the fruit clusters are still plump and tight and juicy. The long season has allowed an accumulation of flavors. "This Chardonnay is going to make great still wine," says Forrest. We walk into block C, which gets the last rays of sunshine at the end of the day. It usually makes our favorite lot of Chardonnay. The grapes from some vines taste like cinnamon and nutmeg; others are more tropical, like bananas and pineapple. Chardonnay is loaded with a hundred different identified and cataloged tastes and smells, which we describe by association. This is not just imagination or poetic metaphor. In a lab, a grape can be analyzed to reveal the same esters or

chemical compounds as the various sensory connections that come to mind; for example, the same esters as green apples if you find a green-apple flavor.

The way we make Chardonnay has changed over the years. When the vines were young, we fermented the juice in stainless-steel refrigerated tanks. Wood would have overpowered the fruit. As the vines matured, their roots extended, picking up more nutrients, more flavor, out of the ground. Forrest began experimenting with different kinds of barrels, various strains of yeast, malolactic fermentation, which changes the acid balance in the grape, skin contact, and extended time on the lees—all are different ways of enriching the wine. Such techniques impart distinctive smells and flavors, affecting the style of the wine. The trick is finding the right combination that best complements the inherent flavor of the grapes from our land.

One of the objectives is to bring forth the natural complexity of the grape—polishing the various facets so that the whole is balanced but each angle can shine individually when matched with a particular food. Like an abstract painting. If you stand in front of a Jackson Pollock wearing a blue shirt, all the blues pop out. Switch to red and the whole painting changes. This is what makes Chardonnay so popular as a "food wine." It's broad ranging enough to match with many different tastes. It's a noble grape because it has so much character and complexity.

Barrel-fermenting Chardonnay has become standard. Leaving Chardonnay *sur lie* is also very common now. The dead yeast cells make the wine seem creamy. *Sur lie* also softens the amount of wood you get in the wine because it is coating the barrels, and the lees tend to protect the wine from oxidation instead of adding sulfur—though in some vintages you can't rely on just that. We leave our wine *sur lie* for eight to nine months. Or at least we've been averaging that for the past three vintages. Before then, four to six months. We only started leaving the wine *sur lie* in 1987.

We used to let the wine sit on the skins before pressing, which is another way of gaining complexity, but this year Forrest wants to barely crush the fruit. It doesn't need it. The flavors are so intense and the texture will be much silkier if we load the whole clusters directly into the press like we do for sparkling. In a vintage like this, we try not to extract anything from the skins and the seeds, which contain stronger, coarser esters.

Our preference is no malolactic fermentation, though it has become almost ubiquitous in many Chardonnays. Malolactic fermentation changes the acid balance, converting malic acid to lactic acid. It enriches a wine, makes it buttery, but it tends to knock down the fruit and give the wine another flavor, much as beurre blanc does in a sauce.

The one thing we don't want to lose in all the technique is the fruit. That's the one aspect of the wine that's proprietary to us, that no one else can duplicate, and which gives Iron Horse its special niche. So that when I call on an account and they say "the last thing we need is another Chardonnay," I can truthfully and convincingly show them that ours tastes different.

We search for that distinctive flavor in our vineyards, but it's very elusive. Sometimes we think we have a grasp on it—it's the lemony or mineral quality, or the heavy content of iron in our water. But then when it comes to tasting one of our grapes against a Chardonnay grape from another vineyard, I frankly cannot tell the difference. Nor can Forrest. There's so much sweetness that you can't taste through it. In the wines, however, there's a clear continuum, a style, an Iron Horse taste that seems to transcend the various techniques from vintage to vintage.

I keep trying to push Forrest into articulating that taste—pinpointing it, quantifying it, tying it up in a neat little package for me. But he says it can't be done. "I keep trying to tell you that it doesn't work that way. It's like a vineyard in bloom. If you stick your nose in the flowers, you can't smell anything. Stand back and let the breeze pick up the perfume and you'll become intoxicated." It's the mysterious part of wine, the part he feels shouldn't be examined too closely. It falls into that fuzzy concept of *goût du terroir,* but a wine can be very expressive of an area—say, a very well-made Chablis—and still not have real *goût du terroir.* A wine made from fifteen different vineyards certainly isn't going to have it. But being estate-bottled doesn't guarantee it, either. In that sense, it's kind of like sex appeal. Some wines have it and some wines don't.

A really bad vintage is rare now. Technology can eliminate many problems such as immaturity of fruit. Flaws can be masked by malolactic fermentation, a little residual sugar, acid adjustments, or wood aging. You can do many things to cover up faults in the wine, but unavoidably the winemaker knows what the wine was like before it was corrected. It's always going to have that "fiddled-with" taste. It haunts your palate. Unlike cooking, we only get to make wine once a year. We get one shot at it.

Our last day of harvest was Saturday, October 19. We ended up bringing in 740 tons of grapes. Almost 42,000 cases worth compared to 34,000 cases last year and 30,000 the year before. We have jumped from being small to medium sized in our price range. But there is hardly any time to enjoy the accomplishment. The winery is filled to capacity. John keeps on moving wine around to make room for each phase of fermentation. Raphael is rushing to finish sparklings for the holidays. Shirley is getting it labeled. Forrest has shifted almost all of the pickers into the winery. Any extras go looking for work at other vineyards. Just because we're through doesn't mean they are.

Most premium wineries are coy about disclosing their production level—like a woman telling her age. Industry analysts say 50,000 cases is the most profitable size in the ultrapremium category. Wineries like Grgich Hills and Jordan are about twice our size. But everyone wants the image of being small, rare, and exclusive, like Pétrus, which produces 11,000 cases a year. How many cases of Dom Pérignon are produced each year remains a perfectly kept secret. The guesses range from one million to two million bottles.

We used to have an end-of-harvest fiesta. Manuel would buy a pig and one of the pickers, preferably one who had worked as a butcher before, would slaughter it early in the morning behind José Luis's house. They would cut the jugular vein and hold up a bucket to catch the blood for blood sausage. The fat was rendered for lard and the meat cut off the bone and boiled for three hours in water, lemon juice, and spices. The skin was deep fried in the lard for *chicharones,* and some of the boiled meat was cooked that way too, so it was crispy though incredibly rich. Manuel's wife, Amparo, made thick flour tortillas, which she brought still warm from the frying pan—more lard—wrapped in aluminum foil along with Spanish rice, mole, and several salsas using different peppers. Her style of cooking is from Guanajuato, where she, Manuel, and many of the workers, mostly relatives, come from.

The fiestas were held in the gardening barn and the equipment yard. The women talked among themselves and minded the children, while the men and the older boys stood outside telling stories and talking about baseball. Sometimes someone would pluck on a guitar, but usually a few people would sing along to the radio. One year, Manuel just stopped organizing the fiestas and we didn't press him. I guess we've just gotten so busy that we have let this tradition slip away.

Sunday morning we woke up to an eerie clearness in the air— like you get from the French mistral, except that this was an easterly wind which usually means fire danger, particularly now when everything is so dry. By 10:00 A.M., it felt very strange, as if the heat was on in our house, but it was just the wind blowing hot air inside.

A fire broke out in the Alexander Valley in the canyon near the geysers, one ridge over from T-T. We could see the smoke from the winery. Driving to T-T, we saw two huge borate-spraying bombers fly over. The wind was knocking tree branches against our car. The air became increasingly sooty. It crossed my mind that this could be serious. "Luckily," Forrest said, "we have a bulldozer sitting at T-T. That's how you fight these kinds of fires. By digging fire lines. Though with a wind like this, fire could probably skip over the lines." Then I realized how harrowing this could be.

We got to T-T and Forrest pulled up at Victor's house. I hadn't been to T-T in a very long time. It was shocking to see whole sections of bare ground where the phylloxera-ridden vines had been pushed out. All over the Alexander Valley you see similar blocks in various stages of being bulldozed. We found Victor on his six-wheeler coming around the barn. After a complete review of the situation, they decided, *"No hay peligro."*

No danger. Forrest and I took off for a wine tasting, a fund raiser for United Winegrowers, at Robert Young's just down the hill.

Robert Young is one of the best grape growers in Sonoma County. Forrest admires him tremendously. And I feel proud that Bob genuinely likes Forrest. When Forrest first started out, he borrowed a tractor from Bob. Bob was already famous for being the first grower to have the name of his vineyard designated on wine labels because of the caliber of his grapes. The most famous was Château St. Jean, Robert Young Vineyards. That was the ne plus ultra. We used to peg our prices to St. Jean's.

His property is in the same corner of the Alexander Valley as T-T, though most of his vineyard is on the valley floor. One day after our harvest was through, Bob still had a ways to go. He was upset about the wind and the smoke on account of the tasting. He said the whole place was immaculate at 8:30 this morning. "There wasn't one leaf on the ground." But now, with the wind, there was nothing he could do. He offered beer and sodas to the people setting up for the tasting. "The smoke looks ominous, but I don't think the fire will come down this far," he said.

He lives in a beautiful white wood house that everyone admires when they drive around Red Barn Road. His family has been farming this land for four generations. The old barn to the right is painted out white, probably the original, but in perfect repair. Satellite dish. Four Port-o-lets for the guests. Rented 8 x 10 fold-up tables covered with white tablecloths, hay bails to sit on. The lawn is perfectly green—what a luxurious use of water!— and mowed to within a quarter inch off the ground. Everybody drove their trucks across it to unload the food and cases of wine for the tasting.

We had one of the best tables—"I knew we would," said Forrest, since he's on the board of United Winegrowers. We were next to the music, a local "big band" playing Glenn Miller dance music.

Right on cue, at 2:00 P.M. when the tasting was supposed to start, the wind died down and the smoke lifted. No one was deterred from having a good time.

Forrest and I took turns walking around, tasting everyone else's wine and bringing back food to our table—bread from the downtown bakery in Healdsburg, which is owned by the pastry chef at Chez Panisse, Laura Chenel Chèvre, and grilled Sonoma baby lamb supplied by Campbell Farms. It was a very relaxed and easy tasting, most of the men in jeans and the women in sundresses. It epitomized Sonoma style entertaining, which, at its best, has kind of a down-home feeling—even on a 600-acre ranch.

The fire continued to burn, but we couldn't get any news about it because of a huge outbreak in Oakland. Then, the wind changed directions to the south, bringing cooler air from the ocean and extinguishing any danger to us.

The Oakland fire raged out of control. Hundreds of people were burned out of their homes. The scary part of the story was the empty reservoirs, which made firefighters on the ground practically useless. The fire had to be fought with borate bombers like a forest fire, even though it was in a heavily populated area. Homes should never have been built in those hills.

Fortunately, there were more volunteers than victims at the emergency shelters. We heard an interview with a woman on the radio talking about what she had thought to save. She said,

"I took the kids' photo albums and a suit, because I have a big meeting tomorrow and I won't have time to go shopping." She also said she hoped her fur coats burned up because they were no longer "politically correct." Fires, mud slides, and earthquakes are just part of life here. As a Californian, I grew up hearing that the state would eventually fall into the ocean and that Howard Hughes had bought up Nevada believing it would be beachfront property one day.

Forrest was at Candlestick Park with his son, Michael, for the World Series during the 1989 quake. Candlestick is a rickety old place and at first he thought it was just the crowds stomping that was causing the motion. Then the light stands began to sway and the scoreboard went blank. Police cars with lights flashing rolled onto the field but he couldn't hear the announcements. It wasn't until he saw the players pulling their wives and girlfriends out of the stands that he and Michael realized it was serious. It took them six hours to get home. The hardest part was getting out of the parking lot.

My grand aunts and grand uncle live in the Marina district of San Francisco. Aunt Bea was actually in the hospital when the quake hit. I felt sorry for Mother—the phone lines were jammed, and all we could see on television was that part of the city was in flames. When she finally got through, Aunt Esther was angry. "Please don't treat us like children. We know perfectly well what to do. We survived 1906." Ninety-year-old Uncle Sam pulled his old Cadillac out of the garage and took Aunt Esther to some motel in the Sunset district, where they had electricity. Aunt Esther remembers standing in the park in 1906, huddled in a blanket.

· · ·

The social event of the year is the New York Wine Experience. It actually takes place every other year—around the time of the New York Marathon—alternating with the California Wine Experience in San Francisco. The New York Experience is the most prestigious. By invitation only. But even the California one can't be taken lightly. A friend of ours from one of the oldest wine-making families in Sonoma thought he'd sit it out one year and he's never been allowed back in. He still attends as a paying guest, even though he can't show his wines, because the schmooze factor alone is worth the price of admission. All of the players are there: Corinne Mentzelopoulous of Château Margaux, Robert Mondavi, the Baroness Philippine de Rothschild, her cousin Eric de Rothschild, who heads Lafite, and Christian Moueix from the Pétrus side of the Moueix family, who has commissioned I.M. Pei to design his winery in Napa. They're like celebrities. Heads turn as they wade through the crowds of consumers at the Grand Tastings.

There's a fair amount of preening to be done at the Wine Experience to attract people to our booth, show off to our peers and, with any luck, get our picture in *The Wine Spectator*. I got all dressed up, piled on the jewelry, and started smiling. This is serious business. We were so busy behind the table pouring wine that there was no time to think. A woman came up to Father and said, "Aren't you surprised I'm pregnant?" "Oh, how nice to see you," he said neutrally, because he couldn't remember her name let alone having that intimate a conversation presumably just nine months ago.

There were 165 wines at the tasting—supposedly the best of the world. Father said that, for him, it's like being a kid in a candy store. You have to get into the spirit of the Experience— you have to pick up the energy of the crowd—taste other wines, talk to people and get jarred, eavesdrop on what other wineries are saying, see who's at the tasting. Everyone has been working so hard it's fun to see some of our friends and chat. And then it's really great when someone walks over to you and says, "I've been told to taste your wine." Every year one wine or another creates a buzz around the room. Once it was the Grange Hermitage, establishing that wine as the most expensive from Australia. This year, the German wines generated the most excitement—probably because they have practically disappeared from the U.S. market. We didn't do badly. We were the first table as you walked in the door next to Christian Bizot of Bollinger. We were pouring our LD (Late-Disgorged) and he was pouring his RD *(Récemment Dégorgée)*. Laurent-Perrier was right above us on the next floor. The whole de Nonancourt family flew over. They are coming to visit us next week.

The New York Wine Experience is the brainchild of Marvin S. Shankin, a great promoter and publisher of *The Wine Spectator,* arguably the most influential wine publication in the world. Marvin is one of the original Wall Street dropouts. In 1973 he bought a little-known drinks industry publication called *Impact* for $5,000, which he published out of his apartment. Since then, he has built an empire. As Michel Roux, the marketing genius behind *Absolut* vodka, puts it: "Now he has us buying five magazines." To quote Michael Broadbent: "Only Marvin could get an aristocrat like the Duc de Mouchy to pour his wines [Château Haut-Brion] at a public tasting." The wine world may be small, but in it, Marvin Shankin is king.

This year was the tenth anniversary of the Wine Experience, and Marvin put on a four-day pull-out-the-stops extravaganza. He hosted a dinner for the top 100 retailers in the business, and at the gala he gave out grand awards for the best wine lists, guaranteeing for the wineries that the most influential members of the trade would be on hand. And as if all that wasn't enough, he raised $648,000 for charity, with a wine auction that was the greatest display of one-upmanship I have ever seen. A trip to California's wine country—including dinner and overnight at Iron Horse—went for $16,000. A wine tour of Australia including airfare and hotels went for $30,000, and, not to be outdone, the five first growths stood up on the stage and flogged a trip to Bordeaux for $45,000, throwing in transportation on the Concorde, meals at the châteaux, and magnums of 1945 from each. During the auction, we sat with David and Judy Brietstein who own the Duke of Bourbon wine shop in Canoga Park in Southern California. David said, "I'm keeping my paddle down. This is crazy." Don Zachariah, who owns one of the most important wine stores in America and is known as Mr. Bordeaux, paid dearly, more than he cares to admit, for sixty-one magnums from the 1989 vintage—reputedly a great one—along with a huge painting showing all sixty-one châteaux in order of rank, like a Chinese scroll. "That'll look great in his store," said David. Restaurateur Pat Cetta made his charitable contribution by buying a collection of fourteen imperials of Cabernet Sauvignons from the top California wineries, each bottled and etched with reproductions of *Belle Époque* posters from Marvin Shankin's personal collection. "At least he can display them in his restaurant."

There was one lot which I would have loved—lot #34—"The Ultimate Insider's New York," choreographed by Gael Green with Nick Valenti, Restaurant Associates:

A Year of Pampering and Privilege, Weekend Bliss, and Late-Night Larks

- You are a guest of The Mark for a weekend in their very best suite, with breakfasts-in-bed and a dinner-for-two in their exquisite dining room, where chef Philippe Boulot orchestrates your meal.

- A glorious suite at the new St. Regis is yours for the weekend, with breakfasts-in-bed and dinner orchestrated by chef Gray Kunz in the new Lespinasse.
- Donna Karan sends you a video of her newest collection, then invites you to the showroom to select the ultimate New York woman's look, up to $5,000 retail.
- Two tickets for every show that opens on Broadway from October 28 through spring, gift of the Shubert and Neder-lander theaters.
- Two tickets to the finals of the US Tennis Open, and dinner at Rackets as guests of Restaurant Associates.
- A backstage tour of the Metropolitan Opera and two tickets to the opening night of the opera season, plus dinner in the Grand Tier.
- Heather Watts, Jock Soto, and the New York City Ballet have four tickets set aside for you to the *Nutcracker* ballet. Come backstage after and they'll show you around (plus attend a rehearsal if you wish).
- A private tour for you and your family of the Metropolitan Museum, followed by dinner in the Met dining room.
- A window table at the Sea Grill the night of the tree lighting at Rockefeller Center.
- A private tour backstage of the United Nations, and lunch or tea in the delegates' lounge.
- Two tickets to opening night of Mostly Mozart and dinner in the Mozart Café.
- A week in the kitchen of Le Bernardin, a visit to the Fulton Fish Market, and dinner for four at the special friends' table off the kitchen as guests of Maguy and Gilbert LeCoze.
- Mario Buatta does a sketch of your bedroom and fills it with his designs: comforter, bedding, curtains, pillows, needlepoint, potpourri, and more.

- Lunch on the banquette usually saved for Barbara Walters, Beverly Sills, and Liz Smith at Le Cirque (where Sirio fusses).
- Romance at Rainbow, drinks in the Promenade Bar, dinner and dancing in The Rainbow Room, followed by the show in Rainbow and Stars.
- You are a guest of the Tisch family for the weekend in a luxurious suite at The Regency. Breakfast is included and a table reserved in your name for "Power Breakfast" on Monday morning.
- The two of you are guests of Mets President Fred Wilpon at a pre-game gala picnic, with two box seats behind the Mets dugout at the opening game of the 1992 season.

Donna Mott at our table pointed out "You could put any product on the map with that kind of entrée," but Father said, "Joy, stay calm. You would need an apartment in New York to go with it." A very fashionable-looking PR agent who represents many of the top chefs of France got the lot for $30,000. Then, topping them all, Michel Roux auctioned off five etched crystal bottles of Absolut, which Roux pledged he would buy back in five years for $100,000. Several people pulled out their pocket calculators to quickly figure the return on investment. The bottles went for $90,000.

Some of the seminars during the day were equally fantastic. Like the Domaine de la Romanée-Conti tasting. The partners Aubert de Villaine and Lalou Bize-Leroy wove a magical tale of a vineyard with a history dating back to the eleventh century. There was a hushed reverence when the wines were poured. That was followed by a vertical tasting of Latour by flickering candlelight, after which everyone got to take home a rock from the vineyard. They had shipped over 1,200 rocks—along with their most exquisite vintages—to give away as souvenirs.

. . .

We gave away Riedel crystal champagne flutes shipped directly from the factory and etched with our marque. People stood in line to get to our table, though some complained when they saw that it was a different glass—albeit a much finer one—than the one we had handed out in prior years. One couple even seemed angry. "We've been building a set and now these won't match."

Our purpose in giving away the flutes is so people will be able to taste Iron Horse—as well as all of the glorious champagnes in the room—in the proper glasses. A wine can taste completely different in different glasses. Red wine is more affected than white. Sparkling wine is the most sensitive. It can go completely flat in a wide coupe and it will certainly taste like a mere shell of itself in a glass that has been coated with different kinds of wines at a tasting. The bubbles need some nick or rough spot they can latch onto and bounce back up to create a crown around the rim of the glass.

One of the tricks of the trade is to etch a little scratch in the bottom of the glass. A few ordinary pebbles dropped into the glass will create the same effect. The tulip shape of a classic champagne flute is supposed to funnel the bubbles. The long stem is so you won't cup the wine in your hand and warm it up the way you would a brandy. Lead crystal preserves bubbles better than plain glass because it's rougher.

The most impressive presentation of glassware I've seen is made by George Riedel of Riedel Crystal. George himself is an exquisitely refined marketeer. He is a tenth-generation Austrian glassmaker, about forty years old, and a rising star in the wine world. He visited us at Iron Horse last spring. He arrived in a gleaming white van, and was wearing gray slacks, a tailormade blue-and-white striped shirt with French cuffs and a Hermès tie. He kissed Mother's hand and lightly clicked his heels when he shook Forrest's. His PR agent unloaded boxes of glasses for the demonstration, while he opened a beautifully fitted leather sample case lined with velvet.

We tasted our 1988 Pinot Noir out of each of his models, from the machine-tooled to the handblown, and compared them with what we use at the winery. He picked up one of our standard tasting-room glasses and said, "You serve your wine in these?" The results were predictable. Afterward we went up to the big house for lunch. I felt compelled to apologize that we weren't using his glasses, to which he said, "No need to apologize, Joy. Baccarat is very expensive. Not the best, but very expensive."

George's father, Professor Claus-Joseph Riedel, designed a line of glassware to be the ultimate in wineglasses. The Riedels produce a special glass for each varietal. He engineered a Sangiovese glass for example, as well as a Cabernet Sauvignon— both glasses that would maximize or minimize different intensities of taste—basically fruit, acidity, or tannins—like an equalizer on a sound system. When wine becomes a passion then glassware can become increasingly important, even essential, like speakers for an audiophile. Gunther Seager, the chef at the Ritz-Carlton in Atlanta, told me it was a question of standards. "Even on a picnic you should drink your wine out of the best glassware," he said.

Of course, unpacking the glasses for the Wine Experience was not so glamorous. There were nine crates. It took us two hours, after cajoling the Mariott Hotel security people to let us in the ballroom before the tasting. Five minutes before the doors were supposed to open, Forrest and I were on our hands and knees in our evening clothes undoing the last boxes, while one of the volunteers stood over us and said, "Are you going to be done soon?"

Three years ago at the California Wine Experience we were saved from what could have been a disastrous tasting for us because of the glassware. Marvin and co-organizer Kevin Zraly invited us to participate in a beauty contest of California's top sparkling wines. The judges were *Wine Spectator* editor-at-large, Harvey Steinman, Robert Parker, whose $35 a year newsletter reaches 100,000 wine enthusiasts around the world, and Michael Broadbent, who in addition to his role at Christie's, writes for *Decanter,* the venerated English wine magazine. Having one wine critic, let alone three rivals, rate your wines in front of an audience is a considerable risk. We got out of it gracefully because our colleagues wouldn't chip in the extra thousand bucks each to rent proper flutes. We couldn't have been happier. The results of the tasting were as anticipated. Nobody won. There was no consensus about the wines. It was laid open that the 100-point scale for wines is just a subjective expression of personal taste. No different from a book or movie review. Or maybe it was the glasses.

Some people in the industry complain that the reviewers are too powerful. Customers walk into stores all the time and say, "I want the one that got the ninety-two." A new restaurant in Manhattan has put *Spectator* ratings on its wine list. At the other end of the spectrum, Peter Granoff, one of the toughest wine buyers in San Francisco, won't even look at scores. "They're meaningless," he says. "How am I supposed to evaluate the difference between an eighty-three and an eighty-four? And I bet if I cut off the scores, I wouldn't be able to match any of them up with the short descriptions that went alongside them."

Before numerical ratings, wine medals were handed out at a plethora of county fair wine judgings, just as if they were pickle competition entries or pie contests. Then there was a period when puffs and stars were the standards of quality. The hundred-point scale evolved out of the twenty-point scale. There are a few wine writers, notably the Brits, who still use words to describe wine.

The best take on the whole issue of ratings comes from a friend of ours who used to be on the distributor end and is just finding out how it feels to be a supplier and get reviewed: "Are we going to reduce all communication to numerical ratings? Someone asks you how you feel, you say, 'Oh, eighty-three,' or 'This day is really a sixty-three.' My wines are worth at least eighty-three. I'm not saying they're nineties—that's the kind of wines you make—but they're certainly not seventy-fives!"

It's inconceivable how much wine is sent out for review. We automatically send samples to some two dozen wine writers across the country. Years ago, Frank Prial of *The New York Times* asked all the wineries to stop because he was being inundated. Frank is very difficult to get to a tasting or out for lunch, so with him it's catch as catch can. No matter who you are. My parents were having dinner at Taillevant in Paris with a First-Growth Bordeaux owner who abandoned them and her husband for two courses while she bent Prial's ear at a table across the room.

Usually, the sparkling wine reviews come out right before Thanksgiving. I am wishing very hard for a 92. That would take care of the holidays. I unscrupulously called the tasting coordinator at one of the publications twice after submitting our samples. The first time he told me the bottle we sent must have been bad and they wanted another sample. What if I hadn't called? The second time he said, "All I can tell you is that you'll be pleased." That pumped me up and I bragged about it to our friend with the bad score, who cautioned, "Yeah. That's what he told me and look what happened. He probably says it to everyone." The most nerve-racking thing is that our mail in the country is so slow that we're usually the last to see the reviews.

NOVEMBER

When we crush Cabernet Sauvignon into the tank it smells like fabulous violets. Then while it is fermenting, it develops a whole new set of aromas, dominated by yeast. Malolactic fermentation has a very distinct, mousy smell. But then, as the wine settles, Forrest sticks his head in the tank, and it's just like the day we crushed it. The violets come back again.

That's when you say you have wine. "It's like the birth of a child," says Forrest. "You have this feeling of well-being, you know it's going to be great. As the child is growing up, you have your doubts but you still have this intense hope that the child will stand on his own. One day it dawns on you that you're looking at a grownup. You shouldn't fiddle anymore. You have to let it go."

It is much too early to rate the 1991 vintage. The wines have barely finished fermenting. There's a long way to go before they are released. But already some of our colleagues are being quoted as saying that for reds this could be the best year ever. The late harvest, three to four weeks later than last year for Cabernet, produced great flavor, while the coolness yielded wines of great finesse. The first inkling of '91's promise came from André Tchelistcheff, one of California's greatest wine makers, a Russian immigrant whose experience goes back to before 1938 when he started making Georges de Latour Private Reserve—perhaps California's most famous Cabernet. He said the potential was apparent before harvest even started because of the long season. Coleman Andrews, who writes for the *Los Angeles Times,* called it California's first "European vintage," because it was so long and cool. "The vintage of the century," some are saying, showing just how French we can be.

Iron Horse has never looked more beautiful. We're right at the beginning of the month. The sun is warm but soft, casting a yellow light that gilds the turning of the leaves. It rained once or twice, but only at night—like Camelot. It is the very picture of fall—our fall. Blue sky. Green grass, so gentle on the eyes after the dry summer months. There are spectacular flaming colors around the big house, where Father has collected a number of trees specifically for their autumn display and hundreds of pumpkins from the garden—some so big you can sit on them. In the vineyards, the leaves on the Chardonnay vine turn yellow. Pinot Noir leaves turn red. Standing up at the winery overlooking the entire property, we can see each block of land—whether it's planted to Chardonnay or Pinot Noir—sharply delineated. We tend to muse about why we like the Chardonnay from one particular section or the Pinot Noir from another.

Bernard de Nonancourt and family—the Bernards, we called them—arrived on October 31. We treated it like a state visit. Four men weeded for a week.

The first night, we had a Halloween party. "Do you think it's too silly?" Mother asked worriedly, while she was setting the table. She laid a white articulated cardboard skeleton down the middle and arranged all kinds of squash and autumn leaves around him. She used two shimmering orange-and-gold Japanese brocade obis as runners down both sides of the table instead of placemats, white china with gold filigree, vermeil place settings, and dozens of lit candles. Terry had carved a jack-o'-lantern that looked like *The Scream*. Bernard was delighted. *"Très original,"* he complimented Mother, putting on a bat mask. He was also very taken with the sterling silver salt-and-pepper shaker crafted to look like an ant. *"Ça c'est drôle,"* he said. He seemed momentarily upset when the houseman took away the masks so the first course could be served.

The two families are very much alike. Language was no barrier and the laughter kept rising in the dining room as everyone piped up at once quite naturally in Franglais. For dessert, our 1988 Brut Rosé was served in Baccarat Grand Siècle flûtes—a special champagne glass that Baccarat named after Laurent-Perrier's *tête de cuvée*. Robert Parker has compared our Brut Rosé to Dom Pérignon Rosé. Few would dispute him, but I think it's like nothing else out on the market today. The color is shockingly vibrant. Most people assume it is going to be sweet. But it is actually very dry and sophisticated. I'm told that this is what rosés looked like on ocean liners between the two wars—bright, almost red, with strong Pinot character. *"Très special,"* said Bernard, which I took to mean "controversial but delicious."

After dinner, we went into the parlor for coffee. Dancing in the parlor is usually something we only do *en famille,* but for some reason, maybe because dinner had been so much like one of our family parties, Father put a roller on the player piano and we all started cutting up the rug to ragtime. Bernard is so tall that when he was dancing kind of a jitterbug with his daughter, Alexandra, the chandelier started swaying. Alexandra is also tall, but other than that she could be my sister—especially in how quick she is to laugh.

We kept Bernard and his entourage busy with two full days of tours, tastings, business meetings, and, most of all, socializing to get to know each other better.

Bernard asked me how I saw the future. I was very impressed that he cared. "The most important thing to me," I said, "is that we stay family and independent." *"Pour nous, aussi,"* he said.

We toured the new vineyard—the basis of our joint venture. Forrest was taken by Bernard's love of the land. *"Félicitations, mon vieux. C'est très impressionnant."* Standing on the highest point—where the old house used to be—we could see the whole property: a "J"-shaped plain cut out of the redwoods, madrones, firs, and some big oaks. At this stage it is a giant earthwork, with countless rows, posts, and trellising. There's only one wire up now—to hold the drip hose—but eventually Forrest will have six wires running down the rows to train the vines, each one strung by hand. We all could sense the potential. "It just has that feel about it," said Forrest. "That it's going to produce great grapes." Though there isn't anything to taste yet. Far from it. We won't release any wine from the property until the turn of the millennium. The rootstock was planted just last spring and because of the lateness of the season, it can't be budded until next March or April. The vines aren't far enough along and the budwood itself isn't ready. About all there is to admire is the take—how few vines died. Whenever you put in a new vineyard there's always some loss to gophers, mice, and moles.

We hosted a luncheon in the de Nonancourts' honor for forty

people in the corral. We had John Cunin from the Cypress Club; Anne and David Gingrass from Postrio; Barbara Tropp of China Moon and Bart Rhodes—who told us that day they were planning to get married; Hubert Keller and Maurice Rouas from Fleur de Lys, and Maurice Neyrolles from Meadowood, so the de Nonancourts would meet some of the French community. Narsai David reported on the luncheon on his radio food and wine show. Mixed in were friends who could give Laurent-Perrier some exposure in San Francisco society. Bernard, ever the marketeer, passed out little Laurent-Perrier pins by the hand-ful to everyone at the luncheon. *"Les* pins" have become collec-tors' items in Paris, and are traded on the Champs-Elysées like stamps.

We served six wines, alternating between Iron Horse and Laurent-Perrier. Father made his toast with our Vrais Amis—which is our *tête de cuvée* and means "true friends" in French. He began by saying, "Anyone who wants to know why I am in the wine business, this is why," waving his arm in an all-encompass-ing gesture to include the time, the place, and the people. He seemed so completely satisfied. Bernard toasted with Cuvée Alexandra, so named for his daughter's wedding. "Iron Horse, *c'est le paradis,*" he said.

The fence around the corral was covered with masses of full-blown red roses. The vineyard was like an artist's study of fall, with colors ranging from chrysanthemum yellow to crim-son. Some of the leaves were mottled and burned, a few still green and growing vigorously, most ready to blow off with the next breeze. We could start to see the skeletons of the vines again. They looked strong. Forrest says they "grew well" this year which means, theoretically, we should get a good crop again next year. During the growing season, we primarily think about growing the best fruit for that particular vintage, but we also have to give the proper care and attention to the vine to establish the framework for another successful vintage the following year.

On November 16, Forrest cut a huge bouquet of roses for our house. The sky was threatening and he didn't want to see them go to waste. "Why not?" he said. "They'll just get ruined if it rains." This was our third (or fourth?) bloom of roses this year. We also got a third crop of raspberries, which were incredibly sweet and concentrated just as the roses seem unusually vibrant. The garden is starting to diminish, so what is still growing stands out as brilliant. There's broccoli, brussels sprouts just starting, cabbage still, lots of lettuce—it's been a great fall for lettuce—the barn is full of squash, onions, potatoes, drying herbs, garlic, peppers, and popping corn. The freezer up at the big house is packed with a winter's worth of tomato sauce, frozen peppers, and some corn. It wasn't a big year for corn—too cool during the summer.

Thanksgiving morning, we woke up to our first hard frost. It melted away at about 9:00 A.M. and the day turned into shirt-sleeve weather, but it still knocked off most of the leaves. Ever the farmer, Forrest said, "This is perfect weather for spraying. Just to get rid of the weeds under the vines."

We all met at the winery to taste some of the 1991 wines. Forrest grabbed a bunch of glasses and a short rubber hose from the lab and we proceeded to go from barrel to barrel dipping in the hose and siphoning off some wine directly into our glasses. It spurted out, splashing all over Forrest. Then he handed me the hose and I got wine all over my pants. By the fourth barrel,

Father was saying, "That's enough. We're going to drink up the profits." Laurence and Terry had brought Justine and Barrie. These two are growing up playing in the barrel room.

The first wines we tasted were several lots of Sauvignon Blanc from T-T. Some of the wines have fallen completely clear in the barrel. Others are still partially cloudy. The first lot smelled like freshly mown hay, faintly of rose petals, and a little bell peppery. It tasted young, green, raw, no smooth edges, youthful and gripping. They've only been in barrel a month since harvest. On the lees at most six weeks. They will stay hard and firm for a few months and begin to soften in February. They are going through their natural processes. Some wines come around quickly and some less quickly. At this stage, the Sauvignon Blancs were inscrutable—so clumsy I couldn't tell anything about them. Forrest is disappointed. They're just not as exciting as he wants. Not part of the continuum in which every vintage is another step up. Who knows, they could surprise us. They haven't seen much time on the lees yet. But Forrest and my dad worry about the combination of a long, cool year with a surprisingly big crop. Sauvignon Blanc prefers a little more warmth and is best, more concentrated, when the yields are low.

It was odd tasting the lots from the seven acres that have since been pulled out because of phylloxera. Forrest can't help making that association. This year, it is estimated that eight thousand acres are affected. Next year, the experts project it will be 21,000 acres.

The Chardonnays were very strong, very intense, very eloquent, and clearly wines with very great futures. We were just enraptured with every lot of Chardonnay. You didn't need any expertise to see the quality of these wines. They had tremendous weight, purely from the fruit. They tasted very lemony, with apples and pears, honey and new wood.

We tasted one lot that was in American oak barrels. Forrest commented that he thought the quality of the cooperage had dramatically improved, but Father was still somewhat negative.

American oak tends to be very strong and seductive, actually very complementary when the wine is in barrel. It adds strong vanilla flavors. But we find that with our grapes it becomes unctuous and overpowering with time in the bottle. Barrel wood in the United States comes from the South and the Midwest, where we find a specific type of oak, one that has long trunks that are perfect for the barrel staves. The dryness of the California climate tends to make the oaks from here low growing and bushy.

Until very recently, American cooperage was substandard. The wood tended to be kiln-dried instead of air-dried, which changed the flavor, and the actual construction wasn't as good. The barrels often leaked. There is still a substantial price difference between American and French wood. A first-class American barrel costs about $200 a case. A top French barrel is over three times as much.

In the garden, things are starting to look picked over. Most of what's left is frosted. We can still find a few hardy fall vegetables—brussels sprouts, leeks, beets, bitter greens. The biggest problem is thinking about dinner and getting down to the garden before the sun sets at five o'clock.

Of course, the deer are happy eating the roses that are left, and an enormous third crop of grapes. The vines are covered with tiny clusters and the autumn has been so dry that they are actually getting ripe. What a treat for the deer; they don't even have to contend with leaves.

Mid-November is also when the starlings return to roots. Six million starlings nest in a grove of eucalyptus trees near Sebastopol. The sky is black with them. And when they change their flight pattern, it's like the sky changing direction. Thank God they come *after* harvest, because when they descend into a vineyard looking for third crop, not a grape remains.

The power of television is undeniable. Red wine sales have shot up 44 percent since the CBS program *60 Minutes* ran a story called "The French Paradox." In a twenty-minute segment, Morley Safer presented the paradox that the French eat cheese and foie gras, smoke like chimneys, and drink more alcohol than Americans, yet have a significantly lower incidence of heart disease. The conclusion from a growing body of medical studies was that drinking alcohol in moderation, especially red wine, reduces heart attacks and cardiovascular disease. The broadcast practically depleted the supply of bulk red wine. A store clerk in Florida told me that all kinds of customers rushed in to load up. "They wanted the one that's good for your heart," he said. "It didn't matter what it tasted like." Safer, now a hero to the wine industry, reported in a magazine interview that he expected a real outcry from the predictable anti-alcohol groups, but he said he didn't get one call or letter of protest. And all of the medical response was approving. However, any attempt to play up the *60 Minutes* report has been prohibited by the Bureau of Alcohol Tobacco and Firearms (BATF), even disallowing buttons that say MAKE YOUR HEART HAPPY. It's a law that dates back to the old snake-oil and patented-medicine days, controlling beneficial health claims in any form of advertising. Many of the regulators are neoprohibitionists. They make no secret of their agenda—to cripple sales with all kinds of restrictions—but it's not surprising. There has always been a strong temperance streak in American politics, one that goes back to the Puritans. Its visibility and force is currently quite strong. We see more and more appointments of neoprohibitionists in Washington, and even in Sacramento. What kills us is when they call wine a gateway drug. One of our original brokers, Tom Heller, told me his little girl came home from school one day asking if her daddy was a drug dealer. Hopefully, we're coming out of the cycle. Very encouraging public opinion polls show that enjoying wine with dinner is socially acceptable behavior to most Americans.

I was pursuing a career in journalism when my parents bought Iron Horse. I got the bug while I was at Yale. I worked Friday nights, Saturdays, Saturday nights and Sundays at *The New Haven Register* as a copy person. I hauled mail, sorted it, ran copy down to the typesetter—the newspaper was just converting to computers—and wrote obits. I was pulling copy off the teletype machines when the *ding ding ding ding ding* of a bulletin came over the wires. It was the "Saturday Night Massacre," when Richard Nixon fired Special Prosecutor Archibald Cox. I felt I was at the center of the universe.

I was supposed to go to law school, but after graduation I drove cross country, arrived at my parents' home—they were living in Malibu at the time—and said, "I won't do it. You can't make me do it." Father looked at me straightfaced and said, "Does that mean you won't be president of the United States?" I had to tell him, "I guess not, Daddy."

I drove back East, to find my fame and fortune in New York. Father drove with me and set me up in an apartment on West 67th Street between Columbus Avenue and Central Park. I had an eight-foot-wide picture window with a view of the rooftops all the way up to the Museum of Natural History. Initially, I didn't have a stick of furniture, so Father sent me cases of wine with a note saying, "At least you won't go thirsty and you can sit on the upended boxes if need be." I entertained in Central Park in the summer. I'd buy a basket of strawberries—which cost a fortune—chill a bottle of Iron Horse, grab a blanket and invite friends to the free concerts in Sheep Meadow.

It took me six months to find a job. I was fairly hysterical that it took so long, but I found out that my type—well traveled, bilingual, Ivy League graduates—were a dime a dozen. At some of the places where I was interviewed, the news director or whoever did the hiring would say something sarcastic like, "Gee, Joy. Too bad you weren't here last week. We just filled the senior vice president's position."

I finally landed a job at United Press International. Again, as a copy person. I worked four to midnight. Part of my job was getting dinner for the editors. When I left the building, I worried that friends would see me and discover that I wasn't really running the place. UPI is in the *Daily News* Building on 42nd Street, near the United Nations. It was built in the thirties and when the heavy steel elevator doors would close, I thought I would die of asphyxiation from the fumes of the "Quarter Pounders with Cheese," "Big Macs," small fries, large fries. The tops never fit properly on the Cokes, so they usually spilled on my clothes.

One evening, the executive vice president, Robert E. Page, III, stepped into the news room. I hadn't met him yet, so I walked over, stretched out my hand and said, "Hello, Mr. Page. My name is . . ." when this blast came from across the room: "Hey, asshole. Nobody gets called mister around here." It was one of the night editors, Lucien Carr. I wanted to fall through the ground.

The stories about Lucien Carr convinced me he ate glass for breakfast. He was part of the Beat Generation made famous by Jack Kerouac and Allen Ginsberg. They say he killed a man and went to work for UPI when he got out of jail. Aaron Latham, who wrote a story in *New York* magazine about the Beat Generation, said Lucien Carr was potentially the most talented of the group, but ended up writing nothing longer than a 400-word UPI dispatch.

Carr was part of the romance I was looking for in the news business—the surly characters as well as the white knights. I invited him out to the coffee shop on the corner once. He said, "Look. Don't you understand that I don't want to talk to anybody?"

When you go to work for UPI, you fill out an application form that asks if you are willing to go anywhere, do anything, and then that's exactly what happens to you. After nine months, I was promoted to reporter and shipped off to Spokane. I still wonder who I pissed off.

I was so totally wrapped up in what I was doing that I was fairly oblivious to what was going on at Iron Horse. Initially, it was this giant construction project, and Sebastopol wasn't any great attraction. It was a little farming town—not quaint, just a provincial backwater with some unusual elements around the fringes: a huge Buddhist Temple, a redneck bar called Red's Recovery Room, Friedman Brother's Hardware Store off the freeway that carried the motto: "If we don't have it, you don't need it," and Windmill Antiques, which put out a sign WE BUY JUNK AND SELL ANTIQUES. Tractor-pull contests at the county fairgrounds were fun—once. It seemed unlikely I would meet anyone with romantic potential.

In 1978, I landed a job in the newsroom at KPIX-TV, the

CBS affiliate in San Francisco, which put me about an hour's drive away from Iron Horse. I came up on the weekends, especially during harvest. Sebastopol was still very rural, but my eyes were beginning to soften to it and signs of civilization were cropping up—like Laura Chenel cheese and good bakeries.

My career track dictated that I keep moving back and forth across country every two years, for better jobs. I was in Atlanta working for Ted Turner when Cable News Network signed on. Ted put me on the air doing "News Watches"—five-to-twelve-minute mini-newscasts between the movies on WTBS. Interstitial programming, it's called. A flexible show that could expand and contract like an accordion depending on the length of the uncut feature film, and which could easily wrap around a commercial or two. I still have a manilla envelope of fan mail, mainly from prisoners and hospital patients. Some of it is quite sick. One afternoon, in Ted's office, watching myself on tape, he said, "Well, frankly, Joy, you're no Barbara Walters."

From Turner Broadcasting, I moved to ABC Network in Los Angeles as an assignment editor. At ABC, we had a joke that it wasn't so much a back-stabbing place—people didn't have time to wait for you to turn around. They'd just stab you in the chest.

I was back working nights again. One of my responsibilities was calling all the affiliate stations in thirteen western states to find out what they were going to use as the lead of their 11-o'clock newscasts. Anything significant would get fed down to us in Los Angeles, and if it was really newsworthy, we'd beam it to New York for *Good Morning America*. My first month at the network, the Seattle station, KIRO, called with a hot tip: "We've get pictures of a duck with an arrow stuck through it." "You're kidding me," I said and laughingly declined to take it in. The next morning, both NBC's *Today* show and *CBS Morn-*

ing News ran the story as a kicker. New York was instantly on the phone calling to find out why the video hadn't even been offered to them. I should have known then and there that network news wasn't going to come naturally to me.

At twenty-nine, I was made deputy bureau chief. ABC was just beginning to look at women as potential bureau chiefs. I went to work at six in the morning to get second-guessed and pushed around most of the day and not leave until seven in the evening. I was utterly unconnected, except for Iron Horse.

The coup de grace was when a B-1 bomber crashed at Edwards Air Force Base. I had five crews on the ground with only iffy walkie-talkie communication. I couldn't get any video, because the Air Force had sealed off the area. I got my head handed to me by CBS, which had hired a crop duster to fly one of their cameramen through restricted air space right over the crash. Frankly, it didn't enter my mind to wave off a military directive.

Shortly thereafter, I got some excellent career counseling from one of my numerous bosses in New York, who told me that no immediate promotions were in the offing. I could stay where I was and if I didn't shoot myself in the foot, I could still become a vice president like him some day. I went back to my apartment that evening and cried. I quit practically on my tenth anniversary in the news business. I was unhappy with my entire life and afraid of becoming a bitter, lonely, brittle woman. I wanted to go home. I don't miss the newsroom at all, though I wouldn't trade the experience for anything. It made me an extremely directed, determined, individual.

I waltzed into Iron Horse in 1985. Forrest made room for me in his office, a small glass jewel box underneath the eaves of the winery, where we sat across from each other at an antique partner's desk.

The first time I was interviewed about joining the winery was for the *Quarterly Review of Wine,* put out by Richard Elia, a Harvard professor of Victorian literature. Every quote contained the word "happy."

Early that next spring my parents and I were invited to restaurateur Piero Selvaggio's wedding in Los Angeles, and I asked if I could bring "someone." The only other winery people there were Maurizio Zanella, one of the first to grow Chardonnay and Pinot Noir in Italy, and the Mondavis. Robert Mondavi and his wife danced over to Forrest and me and Robert whispered in my ear, "Keep that wine maker of yours happy and you'll never have to worry."

Sebastopol still has not changed very much. People tell me there are more stop lights. Main Street went through a brief attempt at gentrification, but I noticed at the chic kitchen-gadget store that they are playing New Age music with wind chimes in the background. The new owner said she wanted it to be "more of a healing place," which I think is too bad because now we have to go back to driving all the way to San Francisco to get accessories for our cappuccino maker.

The Wine Spectator gave us a 91 for our Late-Disgorged, which landed us in their "top 100 wines of the year." *Connoisseur's Guide to Wine,* published in California, gave Vrais Amis three puffs—their highest rating—and Wedding Cuvée two. Robert Parker did not review sparklings this year.

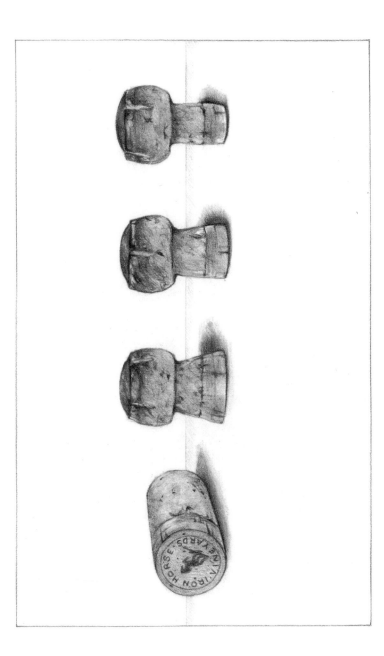

December

The day after Thanksgiving, my parents left for the South of France for the winter. But one last harvest of the year remained: picking the olives for olive oil. My parents like a light, fruity provençal style, which means getting the olives in early, while they are a touch green. Forrest wanted to wait until they were more mature. The debate went back and forth for days, and all for thirty gallons. There were many phone calls from Father in St.-Paul-de-Vence: "Have the olives been harvested yet?" But Forrest dug in his heels. Eventually, out came the picking bins and everybody stopped other work for a short spurt of olive picking. It took two days to harvest our 120 trees. The men stood on three-foot-tall metal ladders and hand-plucked the olives into the same bins we use for grapes.

The closest facility that will custom press extra-virgin olive oil for us is in Modesto, two and a half hours away. In order to keep our oil separate and be the first olives pressed that day, Manuel must arrive at the plant no later than 6:30 A.M., which means leaving Iron Horse in his truck in the dark of night. By 2:00 that afternoon, Manuel returns with the oil pressed into five-gallon plastic jugs. It is green gold but cloudy, and needs a month to settle and soften.

In January or February, Raphael will lightly filter the oil and hand bottle it in clear champagne bottles. There is just enough for a year's worth of home use, and to give to a few close friends.

Napa was a major center for olive oil in the twenties and thirties. Business died off in the fifties and sixties, when most people cooked with butter, then margarine. The resurgence is fairly recent. Olive oil fits in with the healthy life-style of today and a seemingly indefatigable love of Italian food.

Experts enthuse about olive oil the same way we describe wine. They talk about bouquet, color, weight, and texture. Sometimes it seems they are more excited about our olive oil than our wines. Among the wineries, the caliber of one's olive oil is becoming increasingly competitive. Father went to a first annual olive oil conference, held in Napa, and watched the chef of one of the hot spots on Highway 29 try to tie up the production of a well-known vintner's olive grove. "I assumed from the big to-do the chef was making that he must have already tasted it," sniffed Father, "but it turns out they haven't even made any oil yet, so I don't see what the fuss was all about."

The major goal of December is making the *assemblages*, the various blends, of our 1991 sparkling wines and laying them down *en tirage*. This is when we bottle the base wine, and add a precise amount of sugar and yeast to induce a controlled secondary fermentation in the bottle to create bubbles. Then the bottles are laid down in big wooden crates in our warehouses to age. We have 53,000 cases of sparkling wine aging on the yeast. We release about 15,000 cases a year.

Sparkling wine is very labor-intensive and there is no way around the time *en tirage*. One of the reasons it is so luxurious is because the winery does all the aging. It costs a dollar a case a month just to carry the inventory.

We started making sparkling wine because we had so much Pinot Noir—fifty-five established producing acres—at a time when people were very down on the grape's possibilities in California. The dollar was strong, so Burgundies were relatively inexpensive, and Pinot Noirs from California just did not sell. We tried making a Blanc de Pinot Noir still wine, a rosé, in the style of a Coteaux Champenois, the still wine of Champagne. It had a very beautiful light-salmon hue, and because of its austerity and high acidity, it was perfect with oysters but little else. It did not meet the potential of the vineyard, nor our aspirations. So Forrest began experimenting.

Looking back on it makes it seem that we regarded the grapes for sparkling as stepchildren to the grapes for still wine until we came to appreciate the finer qualities needed for sparkling. In the Pinot Noir, we want juicy grapes with thin skins, so we can press very lightly and not extract too much color, harshness, or bitterness from the skins in order to get the most delicate, berry-like juice possible. In the Chardonnay, we want very stylized, restrained, lemony flavors. We use grapes that have a special balance—very good acidity, backbone so the finished wine will mature slowly, and relatively low sugar, so we start out with a low alcohol base wine containing 11 to 11.5 degrees of alcohol.

Our first vintage of sparkling wine was 1980. It was a large experiment. 1200 cases. 700 cases of Brut, 400 Blanc de Blancs and 100 cases of Blanc de Noirs. Forrest made it by the seat of his pants with the help of a young woman consultant, Marty Bannister. They had only the most basic idea of what they were doing. Schramsberg and Domaine Chandon were the available role models in California.

Forrest and Father had gone to Champagne and come home with the latest equipment, but they couldn't get the yeast sediment to settle so it could be expelled. Father flew over the retired chef de caves for Piper-Heidsieck from Champagne. His name was René Menu, and he was seventy-three years old. He had experience with our gyro-pallets, because Piper was the first major champagne house to switch from riddling by hand to the computerized machines. These French-made racks can be programmed to shake, turn, and tilt 500 bottles at a time on any schedule we design.

Monsieur Menu had tremendous wrists and a handshake that could crack the bones in your hand from having physically turned so many bottles in his life. He spoke no English. So Father hired an ex-foreign service officer who was living nearby to act as translator. It was quite a scene in the sparkling wine cellar—my parents, Forrest, Monsieur Menu, the translator, Shirley, John, all exercising with five-pound buckets of sand to build up their muscles. Then Monsieur Menu figured out that the way we had refrigerated the room, with overhead fans, was creating such strong air currents inside the building that the sediment would never settle. We had to tent the whole area where the bottles were stacked. It took two trips—one that lasted about seven weeks and then another time for five or six weeks, but Mr. Menu got the wines riddled and the results were surprisingly good, beyond everyone's expectations. Our first release was tart, austere, slightly green, but it had a certain refinement and length that set it apart from other sparklings.

There is no single champagne taste. Each of the Grandes Marques—the great brands—prides itself on having a distinctive house style that evolved over several generations. We started developing ours with the first vintage. Forrest and my parents would sit around the dining-room table tasting bottle after bottle of different blends with different dosages. There was so much left over that Mother became an expert at cooking with spar-kling, which is kind of a waste because it kills the bubbles we work so hard to achieve, but it's still better than pouring it down the drain. For risotto, for example, she would substitute Brut for the chicken soup.

In the last five years, our learning curve for sparklings has so accelerated that the original vision seems well within grasp.

Forrest says he can taste major elements already in place. His goal is to achieve the richness and density of, say, Bollinger Grande Année combined with a California freshness and lift that goes beyond the effervescence. A richness that isn't cloying. Fruit and finesse. Sweet–tart. "The secret lies in the ying and yang of it," he says.

Now Raphael does all the groundwork. He systematically tastes the twenty-four different lots in every combination and permutation. He assembles four or five trial blends of each of the five types of sparkling we produce for Forrest to taste. Father and I are brought in for the semifinals. The challenge is trying to make it all fit. The first piece of the puzzle is the reserve wine, which we call Late Disgorged. It's our best blend for aging the longest amount of time *en tirage*—which usually means adding more Chardonnay, so the wine will develop more slowly and gain complexity without loosing freshness. Generally, Pinot Noir adds fruit and takes to the yeast very quickly, whereas Chardonnay gives backbone and longevity. It's not just a question of percentages. It's choosing the right lot of Chardonnay to go with Pinot Noir. There is no formula. The best individual lots of each may not even go together.

Next comes our Blanc de Blancs, which is 100 percent Chardonnay and aged four years *en tirage*. We want what Forrest calls "high-point" lemon character—sweet–tart, like lemon drops.

Our Blanc de Noirs (aka the Wedding Cuvée) has the distinct personality of Iron Horse Pinot Noir—berries, plums, spice, and cinnamon. It is dangerously easy to drink. In the last few years, we have added a little Rosé to the wine to give it a slight salmon hue, which in France would be considered *taché*—tainted, in the sense of flawed—but Blanc de Noirs is really a California invention and our style includes a touch of color.

The Brut is the mainstay of the winery. It has to meet so many criteria. It has to have fruit, yeast, texture, distinct flavor, length, and finish. We age our Brut three years: The blend is 70 percent Pinot Noir and 30 percent Chardonnay. We feel the quality of our Brut is the measure of the winery in much the same way that Alain Terrier of Laurent-Perrier told us they relate to their nonvintage as being the benchmark. It's the wine that pays the bills.

The Brut Rosé is technically Brut with 7 percent *bouzy*— Pinot Noir harvested and fermented specifically to add very strong fruit character and suppleness, making it a "warmer," richer, even fuller, meatier sparkling with even less residual sugar than the others. My favorite accompaniment to our Brut Rosé is steak. It's delicious and makes me feel like Diamond Jim Brady.

Bottling sparkling is a sequential process of getting the yeast culture built up to the right point, sugar added to the tanks, getting the blends moved over to the bottling area, making sure that all the *fining* materials are properly amalgamated into the wine, making sure the caps are on securely. It's purely logistical.

The creative part has been done before this, selecting the grapes and blending the base wines. The bottling is exact science—twenty-four grams of sugar plus ten to the sixth power of yeast cells per liter of wine, which produces precisely six atmospheres of pressure in the bottle. The secondary fermentation is one of the factors that determines the size and texture of the bubbles. Temperature and speed of fermentation can also affect the flavor. Too hot and fast, and the wine can be coarse, lacking in fruit, and the bubbles can be gross. Cold, the fermentation could stall, which might make the wine aldehydic: a sweet, heavy, unpleasant characteristic. Forrest wants the fermentation to be perfectly modulated like a bell curve for approximately four to six weeks, to make wine with fruit, finesse, complexity, and countless pinpoint bubbles.

The bubbles always rise from the bottom of the glass. The carbonation is in solution, under pressure, and only gets released when the wine hits the glass. A hallmark of quality is when they form a ring or crown at the top of the pour.

Many people say they have trouble tasting sparklings because the bubbles get in the way. Fine, pinpoint bubbles should help; they gently bring the aromas up out of the glass. Many people say they get giddy too quickly on champagne: there's a myth that the bubbles speed alcohol into the bloodstream, but why complain about having fun? Some people won't touch champagne. "It gives me headaches." That's possibly from too much sugar in more mass-produced products, though I rarely say so because it sounds as if I'm insinuating they drink cheap champagne. I subscribe to all the positive myths about sparkling: that it never gives you a hangover or puffy eyes and that if you keep it cold and put a silver spoon stem down in an open bottle, the bubble will keep all night. Madame de Pompadour, who was an expert on the subject, said, "Champagne is the only wine that makes women look more beautiful after they have drunk it." Lilly Bollinger, one of the famed widows of Champagne, wrote a poem describing how she rarely drank champagne except in the morning before lunch, when she was alone or with friends, with every meal, in the afternoon instead of tea, as an aperitif in the evening, and as an after-dinner drink, but otherwise hardly at all. And as Bette Davis said in the movie *Old Acquaintance,* "There comes a time in every woman's life when the only thing that helps is a glass of champagne."

. . .

Forrest and I made our first trip to Champagne together in 1989. We were received like royalty. We stayed at Cliquot in a nine-teenth-century townhouse in Rheims, which was the home of Madame Cliquot's partner. The façade is still pockmarked with bullet holes from World War II. It is a huge mansion, but there was just us and the concierge, who set up champagne and crackers in the salon each evening and wheeled in our *petit déjeuner* in the morning.

In the course of one day, we were invited to lunch at Veuve Cliquot, raced to a tour of Laurent-Perrier, back to Cliquot to meet Joseph Henriot, the company president, then dinner with Laurent-Perrier's Oliver de la Girandière at Les Crayers, one of the great three-star restaurants in France. We each consumed at least two full bottles of champagne along with more butter and cream than we'd had in a year. I distinctly remember turning to Forrest at the dinner table at about 11:30 and saying, "We have to go home now."

The history of champagne is dominated by women. A blind seventeenth-century monk may have discovered the effects of the secondary fermentation and, according to the lore, ex-claimed, "I am drinking the stars." But it wasn't until the early 1800s that the champagne business really took off, when Ma-dame Cliquot, known as "La Grande Dame," developed the riddling rack so that more bottles could be expedited. Madame Cliquot was a fantastic businesswoman—as were many of the women who ran the great houses and only got the chance to show their acumen after they were widowed.

The word "widow" in French is *veuve,* which explains the *Veuve* in Veuve Cliquot. I was thoroughly delighted when Jo-seph Henriot, in the most charming way, compared me to Madame Cliquot. "Perhaps you are the grande dame of Califor-nia," he said. I practically fainted on the settee, while Forrest looked as if he was going to throw up. That evening, when we went back to the manse, I stood in front of Madame Cliquot's portrait. "I hope I don't have to be fat and widowed, too," I sighed.

The great, ongoing, unresolvable debate about champagne and sparkling is whether they improve with more than a year "on the cork." There are two types of aging with champagne, time *en tirage,* on the yeast, and time "on the cork," which is akin to bottle aging with still wine—in other words simple oxidation, which increases as the cork losses the resiliency that seals it to the bottle. A champagne cork starts off as a full cylinder. It takes 200 pounds of pressure to drive it into the bottle and it immediately mushrooms out. It is impossible to pull out the cork for at least thirty days, after which the swelling starts to go down. Then, gradually, the stem of the mushroom continues to shrink, allowing air to seep into the bottle. When the champagne or sparkling is freshly disgorged the cork is a little stiff, but you get this really great *pop.* A ten-year-old champagne is more apt to open like a bottle of sherry.

The English, who did much to bring about the international success of champagne, prefer extended time on the cork sometimes to the point where the wine becomes maturized and flat. The French tend to like their champagne fresh and lively. Forrest says only a truly phenomenal wine would actually taste better ten years after it was disgorged—it would have to be incredibly well made, perfectly structured, and stored under such ideal conditions to hold up, let alone improve.

This is the time of year when many of the men who work for us take off for Mexico to see their families. They go for four to six weeks. The rest of the year they live like bachelors—sharing rooms with other single men, and wiring their money home through Western Union. They work entirely to support their families. Nothing is left over. Traditional displaced workers. Most of them are in their twenties and thirties.

The growing trend is to sever ties with Mexico. José Puga, Father's second in the garden, went back to propose to a girl from his village but, breaking with tradition, moved her here. Their children are U.S. citizens. Forrest's foreman at T-T plans to go through the naturalization process. Manuel and Amparo Sotello own a home in Graton, just a few miles from Iron Horse, which is increasing in value as development spills over from Santa Rosa. His son, John, who is thirty-six, is Forrest's assistant wine maker. John also owns a home in Graton. Manuel's nephew, José Luis, our cellarmaster, lives with his family here on the property.

Manuel is now fifty-seven years old. He has back trouble. Forrest alternates between cajoling and lecturing Manuel to try to keep him in gear. "It's hard to understand my relationship with Manuel," says Forrest. "He and I planted this vineyard together and he knew far more than I did."

Manuel has always been a kind of wheeler-dealer. He used to run a little cantina during harvest, selling sodas and his wife Amparo's burritos. Most weekends he can be found at the local flea markets. He welds old throw-away metal parts to make sculptures like the two rusty "cranes" in my parents' garden made out of shovels and pipes. He sells Christmas wreaths made out of grapevine canes. His passion is composing melancholy *compasino* ballads about honoring your mother and lost love.

Manuel very often goes down to the reservoir to write music with Luis. Luis is a most romantic figure. He's a loner, and there's no doubt he's had a tough life. One side of his face is paralyzed. He looks old, but he also seems very strong in a wiry sort of way. Luis is a fieldhand. He is also an excellent stonemason and a cowboy poet. He strums his guitar and helps Manuel with the lyrics. Manuel has won a couple of competitions. His name has been mentioned on KDBF, Santa Rosa's Spanish station. He loves to play his tapes for Forrest and Father. Luis gave a poetry reading recently, which was listed in the community newspaper.

December 19. Forrest and I hosted a "sneak preview" party at Red Sage, Mark Miller's new restaurant in Washington, D.C. We had been talking to Mark about having this party for months without really knowing when it would take place. There is no way to pin down when any restaurant will open. There are always delays—getting a liquor license, health permits, and all the other difficult bureaucratic processes. Two hours before the Red Sage preview, the windows were still covered with butcher paper. There was no sign outside, but as Forrest and I reached to open the door we saw that the doorknobs were wrought-iron lizards, and we knew that we were in the right place. A painter was putting the final touches on this fabulous Southwestern mural of wild horses. Plastic was being pulled off the just-delivered chairs. The kitchen was being fired up for the first time. Mark took us on a tour. He showed us seven walk-in refrigerators, a wood-burning oven with three levels of heat—one of only three in the United States—a separate stove just for hot desserts. The scale of even the pasta-maker was unbelievable. Mark said he could feed some astronomical number of people at once. There are over 200 sconces in the dining room—each one is different. Some have silver bullets and buffalo nickels imbedded in them. The talk all over town was about how much money must have been spent.

Forrest and I had invited our usual eclectic mix of friends, customers, and people we wanted to meet—like Johnny Apple of *The New York Times*. His byline is R.W. Apple, and he mainly writes about the White House. He is also a bon vivant of the first order, with an impressive sphere of influence, so last year I sent him an unsolicited sample of sparkling. I was thrilled he came to our party, and when we met he said, holding up a glass, "This is delicious." I was happy to hear it because he had written me that he had popped last year's release with his friend, James Suckling, the London bureau chief for *The Wine Spectator* and they didn't like it. "Ah, but isn't it better to know the truth so you can believe a compliment?" he said. Mark's food at Red Sage is very hot. His axiom is "more chilies"—he loves them with beautifully aged red wines. For the party, he made a beef jerky with Iron Horse Cabernets. "Now, how many wineries can claim that as their signature dish?" he asked.

Unfortunately our political director, Washington veteran Bob Squier, couldn't make it to the party. We are the only winery I know that has a political director. The first time our sparkling was chosen as the official toasting wine at the Reagan-Gorbachev summit in Geneva, Bob helped me write a letter to the president that was a public relations masterpiece to "clinch the deal." Then, the day of the event, breaking the White House embargo by a smidgen, he had bottles of the Summit Cuvée delivered to all the network anchors. Bryant Gumbell showed it off on the *Today* show, prompting Jane Pauley to ask "Where'd you get that? Why didn't I get one?" All of this on the air going into a commercial break, confirming Bob's reputation as a rainmaker.

December 1987, we watched the actual toast on television with our 1984 Brut at the Summit in Washington, D.C. I was beside myself, jumping up and down, while Forrest was sitting staring at the screen with his arms crossed, which, frankly, annoyed me because I thought a little bit of enthusiasm was in order. Finally, he said, "Look at that perfect straw-gold color. The constant stream of tiny pinpoint bubbles." He had been analyzing the wine.

We had the chance to sell out five years ago. In 1986, Father was approached by a middleman for an anonymous client who wanted to buy Iron Horse, causing us to reassess our lives. Who knew when another opportunity would come along? This was at the top of the wine market. Clos du Bois had just sold for $40 million. The dollar signs were dancing before our eyes and, while we didn't know what lay ahead, Father had a premonition that the cycle was turning down. "What if the future isn't so rosy? What if the wine business suddenly gets hard?" he cautioned. "It would be dumb to change our minds down the road for less money."

We sat down as a family to decide our future. I can't remember exactly when the conversation took place but we were in the library where the family usually gathers. There hasn't been room for anything new on the shelves for years—they're crammed with books and memorabilia, including an autographed photograph of JFK, though, sadly, the signature is fading from the sunlight; a photo of Pat Brown dedicated to Mother, from when she was California Fair Employment Practices Commissioner, and of Lloyd Bentsen, signed "To Barry—my favorite grape picker." Circling the room just below the ceiling are Picasso ceramic plates, which Mother bought when we lived in France. Picasso ceramics come from Valauris in the hills behind Cannes in the South of France—we had a summer home just minutes from there. Picasso made limited editions of each plate, which all have different faces—we used to use them as dessert plates. Now they're up on the wall.

Father said that he and Mother could easily retire and live out their years quietly in the South of France. I was flabbergasted. We weren't done at Iron Horse yet. We still had so much we could accomplish. I had just become a partner, and Forrest said there wasn't anything else he wanted to do. We were wildly in love and totally caught up in the romance of living and working together.

The strategy we laid down that day is now coming to fruition. We have taken our wine making up to another plateau on the deeply held conviction that no matter what happens in the world, quality will out. We reduced our yields in the vineyards to get more concentrated flavors. We bought a new state-of-the-art press, reducing our yield even further, to get the most delicate juice. We pushed the aging of our sparkling wines to the extent that we are still releasing less wine than we produce. We created a set of expectations for ourselves. Put our hearts, our souls, and every penny we had into it. Even Father was surprised by how much cash a winery can suck up.

Everything Father predicted came true, and then some. In 1988, we lost 40 percent of our crop. Weather fluctuations that spring knocked off the buds before the fruit could set. Our bills didn't go down 40 percent and though the quality of the vintage was excellent it has taken us three years to make up the loss. A tax increase and a war in the Persian Gulf came at the beginning of 1991. It has been an endurance race ever since. I end each day thinking we've surely hit the bottom, only to have some new disaster befall us in the morning. There was an article in the paper quoting Louis Foppiano that the Bank of America had refused to renew his winery's loan after a twenty-five-year business relationship. The banks are nervous. Three wineries have filed for bankruptcy. Restaurant closings fill a regular column in *Food Arts,* a professional chef's magazine. Deals are everywhere. Apart from the fact that there is an international recession in full bloom, we are also an industry under attack. We suffer all kinds of regulations, taxation, and health questions because there's alcohol in our product. It makes me so mad that we're being hit when we should be basking in the glory of the quality of the wines we are releasing.

Taking nothing for granted, I am getting myself in gear to personally call on every one of our key customers to make sure we don't lose any ground. Like perfume, we should do our greatest business—especially with the sparklings—around the holidays. I can't even think about taking time off until the ball drops and I can't squeeze in any more sales. If there's any business going on out there, it might as well be ours.

A businessman named Eli Jacobs once told me that you should never fall in love with a company because it blinds you as to when you should sell. But this is a life none of us wants to give up. Fighting for what we believe in makes even recession seem romantic, and I have come to realize that no amount of money can replace what we have here.

December 24. Forrest and I are going into hibernation for the holidays. My parents are in the South of France. The seed catalogs are piling up on Father's desk in the office. There is a very forlorn look to their house. It shows that they have been gone for a little over a month now. There's the feeling of sheets covering the furniture. Valuables have been put away; the house has been stripped down, and the cabinets locked. The cupboards are sort of bare; the refrigerator empty. It's interesting how fast a house atrophies. They won't be home until mid-February, in time for little Barrie's birthday. The New Year at Iron Horse doesn't really start until then; it's more along the lines of the lunar calendar.

DORMANCY
AND RENEWAL

JANUARY

THE technical name for this phase in the cycle is quiescence. The vines are dormant; they are storing up enough carbohydrates to push out the buds when the temperatures warm up. Visitors this time of year are rare. Sales traditionally drop to 50 percent of what they were in December. Last January our pipes froze and cracked, and for two weeks we didn't have water. Generally, this is a good time to leave. We usually take off after Forrest gets the pruning underway and I have mailed out the allocations for the new year.

The most fundamental care a vine requires is winter pruning. A few years of neglect, and vines will return to their wild state. It happened at Iron Horse during the recession of 1974–75. Rod Strong couldn't exercise his option on the property, and the vineyard reverted to a consortium of doctors and dentists from Orange County who, after they lost their tax shelter, didn't want to spend another penny. Forrest tried to prune the vineyard himself. "I'd get so discouraged," he said. "I'd get to maybe three hundred vines in a day and there were over eighty thousand—you can just imagine how my hands ached at the end of the day." It took Forrest and my parents three years to repair the damage.

Untrained, a grapevine is a climber. It will run along the ground and spread like wild berry bushes. It becomes invasive and can latch onto trees with its tendrils. Its ancestor, a broad-leafed liana called *Ampelocissus,* goes back to the time and terrain of the tyrannosaur. The wine grape, *Vitis vinifera,* came into being sixty million years ago.

The Bible says Noah planted the first vineyard. He probably trained the vines over an arbor. That's how they are depicted in Egyptian tomb paintings, and was most likely the prevailing theory for thousands of years as to how to get the best crop. Vineyards all over the world are still tended that way, and every other system is just a variation on the theme—whether it's in France, where they traditionally prune vines close to the ground for warmth, or California, where we train them four or five feet off the ground. The basic goal is the same—to find a balance between quality and quantity.

The vines look unruly without leaves, canes shooting off in all directions, but pruning brings them back into line. As each block is finished, we get a false sense of control, as though we made the rows, the wires, and the posts all conform to neat geometric patterns. It will take eight to ten men three months to prune Iron Horse and T-T. It is dark, cold, and damp at 7:00 A.M. when they start. The men create their own fog bank as they move down the rows. Forrest says he can hear the cuts before he can see where they are working. It rains half the month, imposing many days off when the men do not get paid. On clear days, we add an extra hour of work, or we work all day Saturday. Forrest lets Manuel decide. He knows we do not want to incur extra hours, but at the same time the men have families and they need to work forty hours a week.

. . .

Each man has his own favorite pruning shears. They are like a carpenter's hammer or a chef's knives—tools of the trade. The best are forty-dollar Felco shears from Switzerland. Pruners are very protective of their shears, and keep them sharp and well oiled so they can make hundreds of cuts a day. Forrest meters the pace, taking into account inevitable rain delays this time of year, so the whole vineyard will be done when the buds come out in March. The crews start on the blocks Forrest wants to come out first—usually block C of Chardonnay near our house, because it's one of the warmest spots on the property. It's high and well drained, so it's also not as muddy, making it easier to get through. Forrest holds back on the Pinot Noir, delaying bud break as long as possible to minimize the threat of frost and disease like phomopsis, especially in low-lying areas.

The two main ways to prune are known as cordon and cane pruning. Cordon pruning looks as if two permanent arms are gracefully extended out of the trunk along the trellis wire. Cane pruning creates new arms each vintage from last year's wood. Pinot Noir is normally more successful using a cordon or modified cordon system, while Chardonnay is generally more fruitful on a cane system. Cordon is usually easier, because there are fewer decisions. Cane pruning takes more expertise as we have to choose which shoots to use out of ten or so possibilities. In the original vineyards at Iron Horse and T-T, all of the vines were cane pruned, following the theory of the day from U.C. Davis. Now, we mix cane and cordon. The new vineyards we planted in 1986 are on quadrilateral cane pruning—four arms instead of two—which was designed to spread out the leaf canopy, allowing more sunlight to filter through to the grapes and air to circulate around the clusters. The basic object in pruning is to match the amount of wood the vine puts out to how much fruit we want it to carry so the vine is balanced.

Leaving too much wood might result in an oversized crop that the vine might not have the energy to ripen. Leave too little wood, and the vine might grow excessively, diverting energy away from the grapes, which could be a problem even the following year if there isn't enough fruiting wood.

The crew is split in half, with three men pruning the original vineyard. This requires skill, but not the creativity that the other three put to pruning and training our young vineyards. Since they are still in the developmental stage, these vines need far more thought and care so they will be properly formed for the rest of their lives. The crew takes special pride in having mastered a new pruning and training system. There are dozens of new trellising systems being used today. The aim is to get perfectly mature fruit without sunburn or turning to raisins, and without having the acidity drop off or the Ph rise—all conditions that create imbalances in the juice that would have to be corrected in the winemaking.

The first three to five years—the formative years—in a vineyard are the most critical. Thereafter, as long as we maintain it, it is easy to see from vine to vine where to cut to bring it back to form. They are like the girders of a building. Each year, we cut back to the framework. Once a vineyard is structured a certain way, it is very difficult to retrofit it to a new system.

Pruning grapevines is very similar to pruning roses. The cuts take the same kind of strength, as well as the ability to judge each vine individually, but the scope of the vineyard is daunting. One block may have eight thousand vines, spaced four to eight feet apart on rows half a mile long. Even for the most experienced, it takes at least ten minutes to prune a grapevine. As the day progresses, the men start peeling off layers of clothes, hanging jackets and sweaters over the trellis wires. Each pruner works his own row. The faster ones help out the others. The rule is that no one starts a new row until everyone is ready. That sets the pace, and working as a group keeps it moving.

Allocating wine is the most creative thing I do. It takes me two or three full days to do the calculations. I review each distributor's performance, taking the percentage of business they represented last year and use that as the percentage of wine I will allocate for them to sell in this calendar year. Such a strict interpretation of allocations is based on having universally acclaimed wines and more demand then we can satisfy. In reality, the numbers have to be flexible—California could get thumped by the tail end of the recession, in which case we might have to shift wine to Texas and Florida which are rebounding. How to do that without losing our allure requires a certain amount of guile, the kind of stuff we learned in high school about playing hard to get. Our accounts manager, Patricia Chamberlain, coyly puts our distributors on hold for a few minutes when they call asking for more Wedding Cuvée, so that she doesn't sound too anxious.

Another theory of allocations is that they are supposed to be motivating—giving more wine as a reward to a market that's growing and less to states where sales are down as kind of a warning shot. There's a risk that the latter will backfire. Salesmen become afraid to sell something that's too tightly allocated. It's embarrassing not to be able to keep a good customer supplied, because then they might stop selling our wine altogether, sending us into a death spiral of lower and lower allocations and even lower sales. Instead of being sold out, the opposite problem of sitting on inventory occurs, and allocations suddenly become sales goals.

Each state has a natural level of wine consumption. For example, Connecticut would represent 2 percent if it were calculated on a per-capita basis, but because of its level of sophistication it should represent 3 percent of our production. For one major market, I picked a completely arbitrary number of 10 percent. Then I sent our wine manager some alternative numbers. He circled what he thought he could do and sent them back.

IRON HORSE ALLOCATIONS
JANUARY 1992

SAMPLE MARKET

CURRENT RELEASES

Wine	Allocation
1988 Brut	350
1987 Blanc de Blancs	100
1990 Fumé Blanc	limited
1990 Chardonnay	327
1988 Cabernets	267

Wine	Release Date	Allocation
1989 Wedding Cuvée	May	311
1989 Brut	September	750
1987 Late-Disgorged Brut	October	72
1988 Blanc de Blancs	January 1993	80
1989 Brut Rosé	October	100
1991 Fumé Blanc	April	600
1991 Chardonnay	September	640
1989 Cabernets	September	412

It all really boils down to a negotiation of how much each distributor commits to buy and sell—you have to be very careful with these guys when it comes to the differences between purchases and depletions. They can be ambiguous about how much inventory they are willing to carry and how much focus they are willing to put on the brand to make sure it sells through, though in fairness what we are willing to commit in terms of working the market is also part of the equation.

Tasting new wines at this stage is normally reserved for the producers. The First Growths in Bordeaux don't allow their wines to be tasted until April 1. Forrest went through the winery and tasted a number of barrels at random. The whites—the Chardonnay and the Sauvignon Blancs from September—should be pretty well settled out. Forrest will ask his assistant John to make one or two adjustments. The whites are really just aging. Because the cellars are cold, they seem more gripping, even more youthful, than they did at the end of harvest. Meanwhile, the reds are going from tanks into barrels.

Forrest has put together a trial blend of 40 percent Cabernet, 25 percent Merlot, 20 percent Cabernet Franc, and 15 percent Sangiovese. The Sangiovese and the Merlot were crushed together because there was so little of each crop—barely enough to fill our smallest fermenting tank. He has sufficient for one experimental barrel. It's so young and inky—spill any of this on your clothes, and you might as well throw them away. The components stick out like building blocks. They haven't amalgamated yet. The Sangiovese seems to give the wine more acidity. "Black cranberry, if you can imagine that," says Forrest.

I find it very difficult to describe the taste at this stage. Forrest points something out and I can only get a glimpse. But I can definitely see how the wine has changed in just a few months. Barrel tasting is an acquired skill. It's based on palate memory, which is a function of tasting past vintages at the same stage and remembering what you tasted and how that wine evolved. The more vintages you know, the more interesting it becomes.

Red wines evolve as dramatically in the making as they do in the bottle. Various stages are not especially pleasant to drink, but it's impossible not to become attached to a wine you tasted in its infancy. One stage that Forrest especially enjoys is during fermentation, when the wine has this great purple robe, a little spritz of alcohol, but is still partially grape juice. "That's the way I imagine people first drank wine," he said. "They probably dipped in as soon as they got the fermentation going."

January 9. Today was one of those typical atypical days between two storm systems. Fast moving clouds in the light blue sky. 62 degrees. A soft, cool wind. Air so refreshing. All of the foliage has receded. Most of the trees are bare and the pruning reveals the dips and swells of the vineyard. This time of year we can really see the lay of the land and how much variety we should be able to derive from all the different soil types, elevations, and exposures.

The pruning is going effortlessly. The men are doing a really good job and the vines are healthy. They grew so well last year that there's plenty of wood to work with and it's not necessary to do a whole restructuring job.

We are also pruning the orchard, the berries, the rose garden, and all the shrubs. It's a strict parallel. The house gardens get trimmed along with the vineyards. The whole place has a very cut-back look.

Forrest and I walked down to the vegetable garden. There was still one last row of leeks. Forrest stepped in the mud to pull out a couple of beets, some brussels sprouts, a cabbage. Not much is left and once it really starts raining, this whole area will be flooded. The barn has potatoes, squash and onion, dried herbs and peppers. Up around the big house there is lettuce and some herbs growing in barrels. Parsley is still alive, maybe a few radishes.

In January, we have our first withdrawal pang for fresh tomatoes. The thought of getting something out of the freezer up at the big house starts to have some appeal. By January, frozen homemade tomato soup, sauce, and dried tomatoes all taste good.

Laurence and Terry have broken ground for their house. It's at the opposite corner of the property about a mile from our house, with our parents in between. It took them a year to get through the permit process. The county was extremely tough, maybe because we have actively opposed development. The house is replacing an old split-level barn that had turned turquoise blue from some sort of copper treatment commonly applied to redwood in the twenties. They are using the barn boards for the siding of their house, which will have a tin roof and be practically all glass on the side that has the view. When he looked at the plans, Forrest said the retaining walls—150 yards of concrete—could support a skyscraper.

The first hurdle was paying for an archeological survey to certify the site wasn't an Indian burial ground. The most difficult was getting approval for the septic system, which, the way it is being engineered, could accommodate forty people instead of the four who will be living there.

Laurence and Terry are both attorneys. Laurence has opened

a firm in Santa Rosa specializing in winery law—a growing field because of the amount of regulation we face. Terry wants to become a judge. We wouldn't think of hiring outside counsel. Sometimes Laurence feels put upon and threatens to bill us for his time, but I tell him, "Do that and I'll send you a wine bill." He is still my little brother and can be as infuriating as ever.

Laurence and I were very close when we were growing up and there is plenty of everything—especially work—at Iron Horse to go around. But you can never be too careful in a family business. One false move and one sibling or another could get fired during Thanksgiving dinner.

Wine country is full of cautionary tales. The classic was when one brother forced out the other, who then went on to found his own, ultimately more successful, winery. They fought over the usual things—power and money. The one thought his oldest brother was a dreamer and spent too much money. It came to blows. Mother and sister sided with the baby in the family. After years of litigation, a San Francisco judge ruled that the ousted son had been deprived of his share of the family fortune, valued in the seventies in excess of $40 million.

Two other brothers present a somewhat different picture. The story is that one, the marketing genius, said to the other, the wine maker, "I can sell every case of wine you can make," to which the wine maker responded, "Great. I can make every case of wine you can sell." As a result, they are the only wine-making family in the Fortune 500, though that didn't stop them from becoming embroiled in bitter lawsuits over control of the family name.

Last August, we were invited to a gathering of many different wine clans. It was as if a dozen family situations were going on at once. Surely Forrest and I provided plenty of fodder for gossip ourselves.

We were seated with a publisher, a lobbyist, and the matriarch of one of the largest and oldest wineries in the state. She had come with her youngest son, but they were seated separately.

The owner of one of the largest bulk wine producing companies in the state—a real bulldog—stopped by our table. Everyone was all smiles and on good behavior, but there was too much wine power at one table and the publisher turned to the matriarch and tried to break the tension, asking, "Why don't you advertise?" to which she threw up her hands and said, "We're here to have a nice time. Let's not talk about business."

Halfway through the meal conversation was at a standstill; the matriarch's eldest son came by to pay his respects. Five years ago, he was ousted from the family's winery and the story was plastered all over the press. As in a scene out of *Falcon Crest,* the mother asked the son "Didn't you know I was here?" "Yes," he said, "this was just our first chance to come over," and he and his wife kissed her on the cheek.

The most recent news concerns a Mendocino family who reportedly sold their winery for over a hundred million dollars. Eleven brothers and sisters were involved in the business. The brother who had been designated president announced they were selling because they didn't like the "glitzy" side of selling wine. Speculation is that perhaps it was difficult to get so many siblings to agree on a day-to-day basis, or that perhaps there were some pending divorces with difficult settlements. The family has retained a thousand acres of vineyard and they clearly made a wonderful deal, but it still makes me sad that they have left the business. Wine is not a manufactured product. Part of the romance of wine is the people behind it. And there is nothing more powerful than a family that stands together. Laurence points out one other very good reason for us not to fight:

"Looking at our statement for 1991," he says, "we don't have $100 million to fight over."

When Forrest and I go on vacation, we pick some place very far away. This year, we went night diving in the British Virgin Islands. Last January, we were whitewater rafting on the Bio-bió River in Chile. The year before, scuba diving off the southern tip of Thailand and climbing in Malaysia. In 1989, we sailed around the Galápagos Islands. We love to be in a completely different environment, particularly one where we aren't selling. Our main desire is to take a break from talking about ourselves.

In Thailand, we even took a break from drinking wine. We drank Singha beer instead. Some places there aren't many choices—a thousand feet from the summit of Mt. Kota Kinabalu, a 13,500-foot climb, it was Tuborg beer brewed in Malaysia, Coca-Cola, or Chinese tea. By the time we got to Hong Kong we were delighted to find a bottle of champagne in our room, making the return to luxury that much sweeter.

In Chile, however, we discovered the world's best inexpensive wines. Even $2-a-gallon Cabernet Sauvignon boxed in tetrapacks tasted delicious on our river trip.

Chile is very similar to California except that the climatic zones as well as the seasons are reversed. North is warmer than South and they are six months "ahead" of us—our winter is their summer, which is one reason why young Chilean wines seem remarkably approachable. In addition to the lusciousness of the fruit, they have more bottle age than the same vintage from the Northern Hemisphere. I had assumed there were hundreds of wineries down there from all the publicity they have generated, but there are only eleven of size. Forrest and I visited two of the finest estates—Errazuriz Panquehue and Los Vascos—hoping to learn how the Chileans can deliver such good wine for less money than it costs us for packaging alone.

Errazuriz Panquehue is fifty miles north of Santiago in the Aconcagua Valley. The winery is Spanish-Colonial style, with adobe walls and a tile roof. Their vineyards are naturally irrigated by the snow melt from the Andes. It was like going back in time. They still use horse-drawn plows alongside tractors, and most of the fieldhands come to work on bicycles. Pickers are paid about seventeen cents a basket during harvest. Cellar workers get $7 a day and, as befitting their more prosperous status, ride horses to work. At home, our employees get paid about $8 an hour. In France, both cellarworkers and vineyard workers get paid about the same, plus $4 an hour that goes to the government for Social Security. It is very difficult to find a French peasant anymore. In Chile, as we headed for the river, Forrest and I saw unpasteurized milk being delivered to the villages in galvanized steel canisters by horse-drawn carriage. Small children waited in front of their houses with pots to collect the milk so it could be boiled. Construction is underway to dam the Bio-bió in order to provide electricity to these villages; the boatmen on our trip naturally opposed this because it will harness one of the wildest rivers in the world, but Chile is too busy catching up to worry about such leisure-time adventure, which attracts only a few hundred crazy Americans two months out of the year.

The Los Vascos Winery is south of Santiago, where the climate is cooler and the terrain more verdant. The owner, Jorge Eyzaguirre, invited us to see his valley. I thought he meant "his valley" the way Green Valley is "our valley," but he actually owns five square kilometers. The property has been in his wife's family since the eighteenth century. It was confiscated by the Allende government, and they have bought it back piece by piece under the current political regime. Mr. Eyzaguirre told us that because of this process of reinstating private ownership land value is just getting established, and that the cost of labor is also rising as the export market for Chilean produce expands. "I have lemon groves that are ready to be harvested," he said, "and I have to pay a premium to get a full complement of pickers."

Los Vascos is a joint venture between the Eyzaguirre family and the Rothschilds of Château Lafite. The winery is basically a shed, but it houses all-new Lafite barrels. "Everyone thinks our Cabernets are miraculous for seven dollars a bottle," said Mr. Eyzaguirre, "but why do we have to be stuck making inexpensive wine?" He sounded very much like a California winemaker of twenty years ago, with the same vision, enthusiasm, and ambition, along with the same dilemma of how to get the world to accept and pay for quality. Ironically, Los Vascos is not available in Chile. It is for export only. "Chileans would never pay so dearly for wine," he said. "For them, wine is just a generic drink."

Chile's vineyards have never been hit by phylloxera; the vines are planted on their own roots instead of being grafted. The advantages are the speed with which new vineyards come into production, and the amount of crop they can carry. Some Chilean growers brag that they can get a staggering twenty-six tons to the acre, though to attain good quality they have to prune severely to cut down their yields. We feel four tons to the acre is abundant.

In 1991, Chile unseated Germany as the third biggest wine exporter to the United States behind France and Italy. Forrest

concluded we shouldn't even try to compete on price. "We just have to make better wines," he said, "and that means not just technically proficient wines, but distinctive wines."

February

We wake up and there is nothing we can do in the vineyard and nothing is happening in the winery, so we luxuriate in bed for as long as we feel like it, listening to the rain beat on the roof. The sound of cars is muted and there's nobody in the fields around the house. It's very private. It's even unusually quiet in the office. Everyone seems more contemplative when it's raining.

Manuel and Victor check the water gauges morning and evening. José Luis puts out the ALTERNATE ROUTE sign where the creek is flooded, and makes sure the ditches and drains are clear so we do not get flooding in the vineyards. Victor calls to say we are getting run off at T-T and hopefully enough water in the reservoir to get us through the next growing season. February is usually our wettest month. Only the intrepid bother to visit. For us, it is a month of planning and assessment. It's a transitional period, when the proportion of green to brown increases daily. The natural tendency is to look both backward and ahead.

For years, before my parents bought the land that connects Iron Horse to the back road, they would have to decide if they wanted to be flooded in or flooded out. They once got stuck trying to leave for Europe. In a panic to get to the airport, they loaded up a jeep with all their luggage—six or seven huge bags because they were going away for the winter—and had Manuel hook them up to the back of a tractor. My parents sat in the back seat with their houseman, George, behind the wheel as Manuel towed them through the mud and across what was the Snyder property to get out.

We now have an alternate route—out Thomas Road—though it is not infallible. My first winter at Iron Horse, a low-lying bend on the way out was flooded. A county road sign said DANGER FLOODING, but I ignored it, feeling invincible in a huge four-wheel drive GMC—not that I was sure how to get it into four-wheel drive. John had seen me take off and chased after me, honking and hoping I'd stop. "Oh my God," he said as he watched me sink into what was obviously a very deep river. I realized I was in trouble when I felt water lapping around my feet. The truck stalled. I turned the ignition, sucking water directly into the diesel engine through the radiator, destroying the engine. George, already near retirement age but having survived two ships being sunk under him in WWII, carried me to dry ground in front of a sizeable audience on both banks. Manuel mounted another towing operation to rescue the truck. It was months before I lived it down.

Last year a new vineyard was planted at that same bend where I flooded the engine. Driving by it the other day, Forrest laughed and said, "I wonder when we'll see the FOR SALE sign." Vines don't like wet feet—they are prone to disease and tend to grow more leaves than grapes. The resulting wines often have a vegetative quality that comes across in Cabernet as green beans or bell peppers, and in Chardonnay as grass and wet hay. Low-lying vineyards near creek beds tend to change hands in drought years.

Iron Horse has come a long way in a short time. We've grown from five to forty thousand cases, from one winery building to five. The palms leading to my parents' house and to the winery stand thirty feet fall. The place is firmly established.

So far, it has been nice having the broad umbrella of French prices. Their costs for grapes and labor are very high and the exchange rate is in our favor. Transportation is the smallest factor in pricing. In fact, French wines are just as expensive in France as they are here—only here they're not selling. To make matters worse, holding inventory is the biggest multiplying factor in wine pricing, and there is more inventory on hand than anyone wants or needs. The talk on the street is that French prices are going to collapse. During the current round of GATT negotiations, our government threatened to retaliate for trade barriers on soybeans by imposing an import tax on champagne and Cognac. That would increase the price of those items, but the ploy may have backfired. Reacting to the threat, a number of distributors brought in a year's supply of French wines now sitting in inventory. Our wine manager in New Jersey told me he couldn't order more than seventy cases of Iron Horse this month because they didn't have room in their warehouse. (That's the first time I've heard that excuse.) French champagne, in particular, seems to be stacking up. It's as though people the world over no longer feel like celebrating. I'm concerned there's a correlation between the economy, falling hemlines, and champagne.

Phylloxera is worse than we expected. It is spreading at an exponential rate. The damage estimates in Napa and Sonoma range from $500,000,000 to a billion dollars, ravaging 26,000 acres of prime vineyard land once it runs it course. The saddest part is that it won't be over quickly. We'll be in this mode of pulling out and replanting for at least seven years. And the net result may be that agricultural property may be given up to development.

Forrest is resigned to the loss at T-T. "We're out of the denial phase," he says. He has ordered the rootstock for the seven acres he is replanting this spring. It's amazing how quickly a vineyard can be pulled out after all the years that went into it. He is prepared to yank out another ten acres after harvest. An aerial photograph shot with an infrared camera shows where. Everything that looks bright red is vigorous and green. The places where the color is pale green and spotty has phylloxera. "I kept hoping it would just stop," he says, "but it hasn't." Inevitably his entire vineyard will be affected.

Forrest is trying to save at least a few years by grafting young vines to new rootstock before phylloxera gets to them. It's still very experimental and reportedly only effective in young vineyards. How much he regrafts depends on how many vines he can secure. It takes a special rootstock with one long shoot growing out of it that is arched over and grafted onto the trunk of the existing vine. It means spending $2,000 an acre on vines that aren't yet affected but inevitably will be.

Knock wood, there's still no sign of phylloxera at Iron Horse. Ironically, we suffered through several strange diseases early on, like phyomopsis, which Forrest got a handle on about two years ago so that our production at Iron Horse is actually increasing. Normally, we would start replanting at Iron Horse and T-T in a few years. Vines reach their prime when they are about thirty years old. However, keeping a vineyard at peak performance means constantly renewing it, reinvesting, replanting as much crop as we can afford to lose each year. At Châteaux Margaux, for example, they are always replanting. So one way to look at it is that phylloxera is just accelerating the process, but we probably would not have chosen to begin when money is so tight.

I am removed from the phylloxera problem at Iron Horse because I don't see it every day. Forrest does when he goes to T-T. There was a long piece about it on National Public Radio, then it hit *The New York Times* and spread from there. Suddenly everyone became concerned, reviving all the emotions at just about the time Forrest decided to stop grieving. Friends from Switzerland called to find out if we were all right. "Do you have it?" they asked, as if phylloxera was the plague. It's not too farfetched to worry that they'll stop drinking California wines.

February 15. We are hoping for twenty more inches of rain. Water rationing has been called off, but the drought is not over. Apparently the water table levels have not been replenished. We stockpile fifty acre feet of water in our reservoir to take care of the vineyards, the winery, and the gardens. Rule of thumb, Iron Horse uses 100 gallons of water for every ton of grapes. That's 700 gallons—approximately threequarters of our water supply—in two months. By November, we're down to the gray water from the winery. It flows through a screen to catch the solids and then is gravity-fed back into the reservoir. We use it in the gardens. There's nothing wrong with it except that it's a little stinky. The smell blows off quickly.

The houses on the property rely on well water. We may have to drill another well for Laurence and Terry's house, but we're holding off until after harvest, hoping that if we conserve it won't be necessary. Well drilling is a major undertaking, and so far we've only struck water three out of seven attempts.

The most effective way to find an underground source is still a water witcher. We've always hired Ray Peterson—a surprisingly normal-looking person who drives a Ford pickup and owns a well-digging company. He uses a willow twig that shakes when it detects water. Ray starts walking in one direction and if he doesn't feel anything, heads in another, holding out the branch until it quivers. He doesn't make any guarantees. He just points out a spot and for lack of any better evidence that's where we drill.

The three successful wells are near our house—east of the creek, which has meant pumping water uphill to José Luis's house, my parents' house, Raphael's house, and where Laurence and Terry are building. It's a double hop. There's a relay pump halfway up, which doubles the odds of a pump breaking down. Only once have we found water on the west side of the creek, and that was unintended; it was where Father had built a stone stairway in the garden, right across a natural spring that never seems to stop leaking down the steps.

There are many feast days in February, beginning with my birthday which is a major celebration on the order of an intergalactic holiday.

I like to celebrate my birthday in different cities. This year, I had a cocktail party in a suite at the Regency Hotel on Park Avenue in New York, made all the more swank by a holdup at the hotel that morning. Three armed gunmen locked the employees in a storeroom and cleaned out the safe deposit boxes. Arriving at my party, Fred Ferretti and his wife, Elaine Foo, said they had refused to give up their coats in the lobby because they were afraid they wouldn't get them back.

Matthew Green, our wine manager in New York, was accosted by the police when he tried to deliver the wine for the party. I would have just walked it through the lobby, but Matthew did the polite thing and brought the wine around to the loading dock. The police pounced on him because the crooks had been described as gentlemen in beautifully tailored suits. "They had me up against the wall," he said, "I guess they were still a little jumpy."

Last year the party was at my friend Maralee Beck's house in Beverly Hills. Mark flew down to prepare the dinner, which entailed a wild trip through the downtown L.A. food markets. Mark had everyone organized to go to the market at 5:00 A.M., but the place he had heard about, the Grand Central Market, doesn't open until nine. Driving around in the dark in South Central Los Angeles, they stumbled onto a Chinese seafood market that had live razor clams, which have very long, thin shells amost like switchblades, with five or six little clams inside, like peas in a pod.

We celebrated in San Francisco in 1990—the Chinese Year of the Horse—and we combined my birthday with Chinese New Year. This celebration was doubly auspicious because I was born in the Year of the Horse.

Chinese New Year's is still a very real occasion in San Francisco because of the large Chinese population. There's a parade with dragon dances, drums, cymbals, and firecrackers that continues until late at night when the foghorns take over. It falls between January 21 and February 19 and traditionally marks the return of the sun—the beginning of the agricultural year.

All Chinese celebrations center around food. For New Year's, the object is to impress the gods and ancestors with such bounty that they will continue to deliver prosperity through the coming year. Most Americans think of beer with Chinese food. In modern China, there would probably be Cognac and whiskey on the table—status symbols de rigueur—along with a bottle of

Coca-Cola and traditional rice wine. Here is a menu that Barbara Tropp designed: it combined the traditional dishes that
portend good luck, and also favored our wines.

We tend to think of wine as being essentially Western. It was
born in the Caucasus Mountains—now the Republics of
Georgia and Armenia—just north of Mt. Ararat, where Noah
landed in the ark. It moved with the development of commerce
to Mesopotamia, Phoenicia, and Egypt, then from Crete to
Greece, Sicily, Italy, finally conquering Gaul in the seventh
century B.C. The myth of Dionysus, which describes the travels
of the Greek god of wine, is believed to chart wine's expansion
to the West. But it simultaneously flowed to the East. Persia had
wine until Mohammed forbade it. Wine followed the Silk Road
across central Asia, arriving in China under the Ham dynasties
sometime during the second century B.C., and remained in
vogue until the end of the thirteenth century. Legend has it that
the emperor Hsüan Tsung, in the eighth century, had a hundred
horses taught to dance. Their bridles were of silver and gold,
their manes plaited with pearls and jade. The suite to which they
danced was called "The Tune of the Tilted Wine Cup."

The Chinese Year of the Water Monkey falls in 1992. I'm still
carrying around my horoscope, which says "The Monkey Year
is communicative, crafty, witty, and everyone has an opinion.
But those who are suave, smooth-talking, snake-oil salespeople,
who are quick, competitive and convincing, have it made—at
least for now."

It is predicted to be an El Niño year. El Niño is supposed to
bring increased moisture, which will present a complete set of
challenges in the vineyard, but which will, hopefully, also break

FOR JOY!
China Moon Cafe
Birthday Dinner February 4, 1990

A Zesty Feast For One Spicy Woman!

Hunan Eggplant Caviar with Garlic Croutons
Fire-Dried Pecans

*

Crispy Springrolls Stuffed with Curried Vegetables,
Fresh Chilies & Glass Noodles
Cold Poached Salmon Tiles with Ginger-Black Bean
Vinaigrette
Cold-Tossed Salad of Tender Chicken Slivers, Baby
Greens, Gingered Red Cabbage Slaw & Toasted
Almonds with Sweet Mustard Sauce
Crescent Moon Turnovers Filled with Lemony Lamb

*

Stir-Fried Shanghai Noodles with Manila Clams &
Penn Cove Mussels in a Light & Spicy Black Bean
Sauce with Carrot Batons, Baby Bok Choy
& Anaheim Chili Rings
Pot-Browned Noodle Pillow Topped with Spicy Pork
Ribbons, Ruby Chard, Yellow Wax Beans & Wild
Mushrooms in a Zesty Fresh Orange Sauce

*

Fresh Ginger Ice Cream
with Bittersweet Chocolate Sauce
Fabulous Cookies of Good Fortune

Coffee * Tea * Espresso

We Love You, Joy!
Barbara Tropp * Chef/Owner

the drought. El Niño is a recurring quirk in the normal weather patterns. It is such a complex phenomena that meteorologists didn't put the pieces together until the 1920s. They still don't agree on what triggers it. They believe it starts near the Galápagos Islands when the prevailing winds inexplicably stop blowing, reversing the ocean currents. Without the Humboldt Current churning up cold water from the ocean's depths, the whole Pacific heats up and the warmer waters affect everything, from bird and fish migration to drought in Africa.

The El Niño got its name from the Peruvian fishermen who saw the early signs of the phenomena around Christmas time. El Niño means "the Christ Child." The first time we ever even heard of El Niño was in 1983. A dreadful vintage. Forrest will never let a year like 1983 happen to us again. "You have to be an idiot not to have learned after eighty-three how to cope with heavy moisture during the spring and rain during the growing season," he says, "though now that we know what to do probably something different will happen."

Farming is a gamble. There are so many forces beyond our control we might as well look in a crystal ball to predict the future. Though that doesn't stop any of us from forming an opinion. Mother swears by *The Farmer's Almanac,* which makes no mention of El Niño. She also foresees five years of hard work. "Maybe four," she says. I asked her if that included this year and she said yes, so presumably that's three years of hard work. Then, she says, we'll be the first family of wine. Of course that may be by attrition. Forrest says in a few years we may be the only family in wine.

Father anticipates another difficult year economically. Laurence has his prediction for the year, too: he says it's going to rain in July because that's when they will be putting the roof on their house.

. . .

The selling season starts the day after my birthday. Forrest and I split forces in Manhattan so we could cover more events. I went to Albany for the Desmond Wine Festival—my once-a-year trip to upstate New York—and Forrest stood in for me at Boston's Anthony Spinazolla Gala.

I failed to mention to Forrest that Spinazolla is always black tie, and he never looked in the event file. He took it in stride though and that afternoon bought a new tuxedo—not a normal impulse buy, but the store did get the alterations done in two hours. Truth be told, he needed a new tuxedo anyway, but he still didn't need another pair of evening shoes or another tie or cummerbund.

The Gala's original purpose was to memorialize Anthony Spinazolla, a food-and-wine columnist for *The Boston Globe* credited with bringing up and encouraging a new generation of chefs. It was very sentimental at first. Everyone reminisced about the last time they had seen Anthony. There was a special sense of community surrounding the event. It raised money to fund a scholarship at Boston University's Culinary School and it was great PR having all the top local chefs in one room. The best part of the evening was the half hour before the doors opened, when the chefs were all set up and I could bring a chilled bottle of sparkling and some flutes to their booths. They loved the attention, and the sparkling always hit the spot.

Forrest carried out the tradition, but he said he definitely felt like he was the second string. He said he wanted to put up a sign so he wouldn't have to keep repeating where I was. "I don't know why nobody wanted to talk to me," he said, "I'm just the winemaker."

. . .

I used to think that one person—namely, me—should be able to sell at least 30,000 cases of wine a year; however, this year it looks as if it will take all of us on the road to accomplish our goals. The amazing thing is to think about where we were two months ago—selling out of wine—and now here we are starting all over again with new vintages. It's a race without a finish line.

My parents came home from France mid-month. Their return sparked a brief spurt of activity, like false spring, when everyone ran around trying to complete two-and-a-half-months' worth of delayed projects in a few days. Their freezers were supposed to be repaired and a new floor laid down in their kitchen. Ask them. They'll tell you how nothing they requested got done— even the simplest thing waited until they got home.

Mark is very excited they're back. He hasn't been busy enough and he missed them. We all missed them. We barely gave them a day to time adjust or even halfway unpack before we invited ourselves over for a big family meal.

Our family gatherings are always chaotic. Everyone talks at once, and Max, my parents' corgi, is always underfoot. Barrie climbs under the table with Max, and Max starts barking. Meanwhile, Justine is up, helping Philip, the houseman, serve. Mother says we are like a Noël Coward play about a family in the thirties, who are so nutty and overpowering that they don't even notice when their guests get up to leave—they keep on talking. No matter what. Our friend Sidney Moore says being with us is very relaxing. "You don't ever have to say anything. You can just sit back and be entertained."

None of us is lacking an opinion on any topic. We love to talk about politics. This is a presidential year and at this point a new generation of Democratic candidates, including Jerry Brown and a long shot named Bill Clinton, are tramping around in the snow in New Hampshire. We don't just limit ourselves to American politics. We can have a long discussion about free trade with Mexico: Czechoslovakia—the differences between the Czechs and the Slovaks—the Austro-Hungarian Empire, and the fate of the Germans from Sudetenland.

We gossip. Business comes up, but only in shorthand: things like, "Remind me to call so-and-so in the morning," or "Would you write . . ." Father starts to fret about a V.I.P. luncheon when he and Mother will be away again so Forrest pipes up with the idea of life-size smiling cutouts—one of Mother and one of Father—propped up in chairs at the head of the dining-room table, with mechanical arms waving back and forth. Fortunately, everyone took it humorously.

We talk about the art market—Father follows the auctions avidly, believing it's as good an indicator of the economy as the stock market, and right now he says it's down—except for signed French antiques like their Jacob chairs.

Meanwhile, Barrie, aged two, has gone into the other room and is playing zoo on the living-room carpet, making ghastly noises that lead everyone at table to conclude that the zoo keeper had been put in the cage along with the lion.

Many marketing decisions get made around the family table. That's when the partners are all together. My parents and Forrest used to do their tastings at this table; now, we have a fancy, brightly lit lab, though Forrest still says the dining room is where wine really has to shine. "This is the real context in which it's going to be enjoyed," he says.

We dine by candlelight and down the center of the table Mother had arranged a dozen Victorian green-glass bulb vases—a new acquisition from Asprey's in London—each one filled with a different spring flower. Normally, my parents serve three wines—sparkling in the library before we sit down, then a white and a red. But on big occasions like this, there are many glasses on the table. Everyone, including the children, is expected to taste and contribute their comments. An ongoing discussion of the wines is interwoven into our conversation as each one is served, and then periodically throughout the meal as the wines evolve in the glass.

Father brings out some of his best wines for family. For this late-winter Sunday lunch, he selected Iron Horse 1989 Brut Rosé for the aperitif in the library, followed by 1982 Guigal La Moline Côte Rôtie, 1986 Bonnes Mares Comte de Vosges Burgundy and 1970 Latour. Father said he was down to about two or three bottles of the Bonnes Mares. Wines like these need to be set up so the sediment settles for at least two or three weeks beforehand. He must have thought about this lunch before he left on his trip.

Mark prepared a hearty meal to go with the wines. Lentil soup with meatballs, corned beef and beets, gorgeous cheeses and country bread, chocolate truffles for dessert.

We didn't go into the parlor for coffee, because Mother hadn't had a chance to look in there to make sure the flowers were all right. Even when it's just family she wants the flowers to be perfect. That's just the way she is, so we left that door closed and went back into the living room.

We were all feeling wonderfully relaxed until I decided to bring up the question of completely changing our labels. Even an outsider would have realized that my timing was off. The evening ended with hugs and kisses. Mother was starting to turn out the lights before we even got up. Father's eyes were like slits, though he was smiling. He kissed me on the forehead and said, "We can talk tomorrow."

MARCH

The smell of grass in the air makes our noses twitch and we shake ourselves out of hibernation. The weather is warming up. The buds are swelling. Soon we'll be back to growing grapes. Daffodils are popping out all over. Fields that were bare, brown, and boggy are suddenly green. Hyacinths and crocuses appear along the walkways. The camellias are showing some pink and the fruit trees are about to burst forth. The Sangiovese at T-T is putting out leaves. The whole cycle is renewing itself.

Pruning in the vineyards has to accelerate so we will finish by bud break, which Forrest feels is a couple of weeks ahead of last year. Soon we will be worrying about frost. It dawns on us that the Sauvignon Blanc needs to get bottled and that Forrest and I have to hurry up and write the copy for the label.

The weather changes from sunshine to rain in an hour. I can't tell if the storms are coming or going. Rainbows are almost a weekly occurrence. The only problem is that every time it rains it muddies the vineyards so we can't get in to do any work. This is worrying Forrest, because he wants to get the budding done on Thomas Road before the vines push out too far. He already had one delay—last September, when the weather was so cold the vines didn't grow enough to be budded. The only two times a year you can bud is early spring and in the fall before the vines go dormant.

How can we feel like we're already slipping behind? Forrest says he wants it to be cooler and for his men to work twenty-six hours a day. Each morning, when I ask him how his day looks, he says, "Busy. I have so much to do I don't know what to do first. It's like 'pick a project.' "

Budding is grafting. It's the way a particular variety, say Chardonnay, is attached to the rootstock. First we have the heads of the vine clipped down to about two inches. After that, it's like woodworking: The budder cuts a two-inch long piece of scion wood, notches it, and slips it into an interlocking cut on the rootstock. The two ends fit together like inlaid wood. The budder binds the pieces with a special kind of white elastic tape, so when he pulls it tight it really locks in the budwood. Then they cover it with tree seal—black gummy stuff like tar, which makes a protective cast around the joint. Depending upon how much they have to give up to the contractor, budders probably make sixty to seventy cents per vine. They average 350 vines a day in eight to ten hours of very demanding work, work carried out kneeling and about two inches off the ground. The old-timers carry along cushions to kneel on, and they have helpers who get paid considerably less to shovel dirt. Budding is considered an art. The best crews guarantee a 90 percent take. If Mother Nature cooperates and the weather is warm and sunny for a month, the vines will develop calluses and begin to grow together. The threat of rain has Forrest thinking about covering each graft with a plastic bag. We have 40,000 on hand in case of emergency. They would be put on one by one in the middle of a storm if need be. It is very important to have a solid "take" throughout the vineyard to ensure uniformity in later years.

. . .

March 18. It was very sad when it started raining. All hands were put to trying to protect the newly budded vines on Thomas Road. It was strenuous, miserable work. Luis pulled a stomach muscle from bending over. We lost 4,000 vines, which had to be rebudded and/or replanted—a $10,000 hit, counting all the extra work we had to do.

Visitors are starting to trickle back in and wine sales are picking up. All weekend we were startled by hesitant drivers on the road past our house. We could hear the cars going up to the winery, prompting José Luis's dog, Cholo, to bark and the cats around the barn to scatter. A short time later we heard Andrew's laughter rolling down the hill as he loaded cases of wine into their cars.

Everything is building to a crescendo. As the buds begin to open in the spring, the young wines also begin to open up and flower. They start to show their real potential. They are awakened, just as the vines are awakened. Some of the more subtle elements in the wine are starting to emerge.

By now the reds have settled clear in the barrels. They have the first kiss of oak. They are young wines beginning the maturation process. They have a very impressive purple robe of youth. The fruit is beginning to amalgamate with the alcohol and acid, though it is still very young—extremely tannic—just showing a shadow of what the wine could be.

The Sauvignon Blancs are ready to be taken out of barrel. John tastes them, lot by lot. As each one becomes ready, he pumps the wine out of the wood into stainless-steel tanks. The barrels then go into storage, where they will sit in a temperature- and humidity-controlled cellar until next harvest.

The changes in the Chardonnay lots are subtle. They are

bright, tropical, beginning to show some structure on the palate but still tart and tight, unyielding. They have been in barrel for five months. From here on out the pace of evolution will accelerate month to month. The changes will come much more quickly. Last year at this time we were tasting 1990 Chardonnay. That wine was so luscious and silky from the very beginning and our success with it gives us very high hopes for the '91. The new wine is very similar. Except that, because of the length of the growing season, it's like an accordion that has been opened up to reveal more notes.

The 1991 sparkling wines have just finished their second fermentation. They taste like base wine with bubbles. Kind of a mishmash—both the fruit and the yeast are pronounced— there's still a lingering smell from the second fermentation. They won't be touched again for a year, when each bottle will be picked up and shaken to redistribute the yeast.

At this stage, there is nothing we can do to alter the wines. Their character is set and in a sense, from this point forward they make themselves.

The 1991 Fumé is the first wine we will release of the vintage. It was such a cool growing season that we ended up with low Ph, high acid, but a fair amount of alcohol and full flavor. It's a wine that made it against the odds. Generally, Sauvignon Blanc likes warmer weather. A big crop also gave us doubts about how the wine would turn out. It's still very young and very grape-fruity, which is what Sauvignon Blanc generally tastes like at this stage. Forrest is surprised and pleased that the '91 shows very little, if any, herbaceousness. It's like white roses with vanilla, honey, and citrus. It's very zesty and juicy. We expect it will be very long-lived because of the length of the growing season.

We have called this wine Fumé Blanc since the first vintage in 1980. Back then, all the best Sauvignon Blancs were being made and marketed as Fumé Blancs. The style was varietal, crisp, and dry as opposed to being an innocuous sweet jug wine. Today, the designation "Fumé Blanc" is meaningless. There is no consensus among winemakers as to what it signifies stylistically, let alone quality-wise. Nonetheless, we are staying with the name because Iron Horse Fumé has a following and we are more interested in expressing T-T than a particular grape.

For Forrest, the '91 Fumé will never taste good. Everybody in the world could love it and he would still find fault with it. He's prejudiced against it because it's got "phylloxera" written all over it. It's tinged with disappointment and sadness.

"I feel like I must have done something wrong to end up with a vineyard that's dying," he says. And those feelings get transferred into the bottle of wine. But '91 will close the book on it—on both the phylloxera and a period or style of winemaking which was based on a vineyard that has now been pulled out. The new focus will be a young hillside vineyard and the Viognier that Forrest planted in 1988.

The 1992 Fumé Blanc will be the beginning of a new generation of wines—an entirely new style, which we hope will last more than eleven years. We can get an inkling of what that taste will be from a trial blend from the 1991—one barrel, twenty cases—which we held out with 15 percent Viognier, which is probably closer to what the final blend will be when we get a commercial size crop. The idea of blending it with Forrest's Sauvignon Blanc is to "push" the distinctive honey-citrusy quality we love so much in Forrest's wine.

Viognier makes the most expensive white wine of the Rhône Valley. It is extremely difficult to grow, which is probably what attracted Forrest. It yields a poor amount of fruit per vine, and many vines often give no fruit at all. This, of course, raises costs. An acre of land cultivated with Viognier might never become profitable unless the wine sells for $20 a bottle.

Viognier comes from Condrieu in the north of the Rhône Valley and from the neighboring Château Grillet, a seven-and-a-half-acre property that at one time was the smallest Apellation d'Origine Contrôlée in all of France. Château Grillet is a legendary vineyard. Father and I visited it in the seventies. The property is shaped like a Roman amphitheater, with very steep walls. The wines, as I remember them, had a distinctive honied quality that—sadly—I no longer discern in recent vintages. Perhaps, it's the stuff of romance, but I believe it's in the soil and that a future custodian will be able to revive the wines.

Before our Fumé is bottled, we draw a sample out of the tank. Our ritual is to taste from a little tenth—one of the clear, half bottles we use in the lab. We toast each other numerous times and then write a few salient, tempting lines about the wine, usually while Forrest is cooking dinner at home. There is room for only fifty words on the label, and our test of a great evening is how easily they fall into place. We finish the tenth to celebrate.

There is something wonderfully pagan and intoxicating about drinking young wines. It goes back to the most ancient celebration of Dionysus, when the jars of wine sealed since the autumn were opened for libations at the god's sanctuary. Joseph Campbell drew a connection between Dionysus and Jesus Christ, because the wine god was twice born and also in the sense that the Maenads, the followers of Dionysus, felt they were drinking their god and in doing so would be filled with his powers. The choric poem honoring Dionysus, the dithyraint, is considered one of the earliest forms of theater. Rituals for all the Greek gods involved wine—and symposiums were, originally, organized wine tastings. The festival for Dionysus peaked with an orgy during which the devotees danced themselves into such a frenzy that they would tear apart small animals, sometimes even children, with their bare hands and eat the raw flesh. These gruesome feasts belonged to ancient times and were believed to be linked to the mystery of death and renewal. Artists and poets still find life's meaning in a glass of wine. At the very least it can get the creative juices flowing.

March 31 will be a contender for one of the most beautiful days of the year. The morning started off with a blue sky. A light breeze picked up at about 10:00 A.M., but the sun was just warm enough for us to steal an hour after lunch for sunbathing. The entire property is in bloom. It's such a display you think it must be the finale when, in fact, it's only the beginning. Father caught himself worrying that it was all going to end in a week. "You forget that new things keep coming," he said. In fact, we're right in a transition period between daffodils and tulips.

It's all so sweet-smelling—japonicas, wisteria, lilac, and flowering cherries, plums, pears, and apples are all in bloom. The birds are back to nesting in our outdoor light fixtures and in the chimney in the parlor. Our family of red-tail hawks have returned. They established a nest in one of the oaks behind our house last year, and we loved watching the chicks hop from branch to branch and learn to fly. They were like pets—every morning, we would pull out our binoculars and follow them. For days, I've been instinctively looking over at the trees in anticipation. We are into a new growing season. We have bud break in the vineyards. The frost protection system is being tested. The vineyards need their first spray of fungicide. Everyone is speculating on what kind of a year it will be. At this point, the 1992 vintage is a complete mystery. There are so many variables, so many outside forces that buffet the winery—each year is different and, yet, there is the surety that the cycle will somehow renew itself and we will make and sell wine as always.

EPILOGUE

January 31, 1993. 1991 seems like ages ago. Looking back on it now, it was a real test of faith. Sales were very difficult. In 1991 and continuing through 1992, just standing still, maintaining price and market share, seemed a triumph. Phylloxera took its toll both emotionally and physically, and the lateness of the harvest was a serious concern. We talk about stress on the vines, but what about stress on the wine maker? I certainly was not sorry to see 1991 go, and Forrest was disgruntled that the negatives overshadowed the quality of the vintage. "Don't forget about the wines," he kept saying. "Ninety-one was a great vintage and great vintages have a way of jump-starting the market." Since he is the wine maker, I think it is only fair that he have the last word on the year.

WINE MAKER'S ASSESSMENT
OF THE VINTAGE

1991 was a gripping year. All its uncertainties created an excitement that produced truly interesting wines. It felt like a challenge well met. There are times I want to say to Mother Nature, "See what we can do?" but I honestly believe that great vintages are *her* work—the work of nature.

Wishing for a great year is easy, but proving it is more difficult. I remind myself that I have only seen twenty-two growing seasons at Iron Horse and I doubt if another thirty years will expose a pattern that would allow me to really predict the future of a vintage. This ensures the impossibility of boredom or complacency as a winegrower. With each vintage, I redefine concepts like balance, ideal fruit. Each year I find new elements that change my view, my perception of how to make a better wine in the future.

When we look back at our most recent vintages, 1991 can be put into better perspective.

By comparison, 1992 was a textbook vintage. The El Niño threats disappeared in July. In fact, the *San Francisco Chronicle* renamed the phenomena La Niña, because the weather pattern was persistently perfect. Gerald Asher told me he didn't hear any complaints about the vintage—"I guess that means it was good," he said. The 1992 harvest started early, ended early, and was problem-free, but it didn't have the natural spark of 1991. Nevertheless, we were lucky. A human spark to the vintage was Michael Scholtz, who came from Australia to work the harvest and stayed to help make the red wines. His extraordinary attention will make these wines better than they might have been.

With 1990 came a return to the intensity of the '85s and '87s in all the wines. Chardonnay was my favorite until 1991 came along. The extremely short crop at T-T made a wonderfully intense Fumé Blanc that is just beginning to evolve. The sparkling wines continued on their upward spiral. The most interesting wines of the vintage may be the Cabernets. There are two lots of 1990 that will be bottled in December of 1992. They show the intensity of flavor, the richness across the mid-palate, which I have not seen since the '87s. One of these wines may be reserve wine. I'll have to wait for at least a year of bottle age to be sure. Right now the wines change so quickly in the glass you feel as if your palate is being boomeranged around the room.

1989 was first and foremost a growers' vintage. If you read the signs correctly, you thinned your grapes, opened your canopies, and gave your wine maker something good to work with. Careful wine making has given our 1989s a good future.

The 1988s were a bit of a disappointment after the 1987. Even though the crop was extremely small on both ranches, the expected explosion of intensity did not occur. The vintage has been panned in Napa for producing wines that lacked depth, but I think, overall, the wines from our areas have been good to drink and in some cases quite excellent. Our 1988 Blanc de Blancs will be benchmark sparkling wine for us. Already, with less than four years *en tirage* it shows such elegance on the palate.

1987 was a small crop that matured perfectly. This was the vintage that made me realize that we had so much more potential with both our Cabernet and our sparkling. Almost six years later those wines continue to amaze me by their development and their youth.

Assessing a vintage like 1991 is fraught with danger. Unusual vintages do not always make great wine, but they do offer rare opportunities. The anomalies of this vintage: torrential rains in March which broke the drought; an early budbreak; an abnormally cool September—all played important roles. My interpretation of the year was to get out of the way and let the grapes do the talking. There is an extra richness, a denseness, to the Chardonnays, an extra-exotic flavor when you put the Fumé

Blanc in your mouth. The sparkling wines show an extra creaminess. Reflecting on the wines from T-T, one realizes that it is a vintage of extra sadness, considering that many of the vines making these extra wines have to be removed because of phylloxera.

1991 has the potential of being a great vintage. It is still too early to tell. The wines haven't fully evolved. It may be five years before I can determine whether the Chardonnay has the stuff to develop with grace and guile, and ten years or more to tell if the Late-Disgorged Brut matches my dream of a cuvée to rival the complexity of a Krug Millisime or a Bollinger Grande Année. The Cabernets will take at least that long to come into their own . . . This is my best guess as to where these 1991 wines are going.

1991 BRUT Sparkling wines with a year *en tirage* are still very much a work in progress. However, at this stage I can tell that the wine has the framework, the shell, from which a great wine will emerge. Although not perfectly riddled at this point, I can see that the bubbles will be pinpoint size. The wine seems frothy, but the carbonation is delicate on the palate. That is a great sign, since the longer *en tirage,* the creamier the Brut will become. It is very lemony, showing lots of Chardonnay now. The mid-palate is mouth-filling and the finish shows extra length. All the elements seem to be evolving—not in lockstep, but in harmony. I can't wait for another two or three years of ageing. At that time we will have a good idea at what rate the wines are ageing. My feeling is that they will still be very young but already very delicious.

1991 FUMÉ BLANC This wine has developed seriously since being bottled in April 1992. The fresh, sappy, fruity aroma has been replaced by a very intriguing bottle bouquet with honey, spice, tobacco, earthiness, and white flowers in the background. There is a velvety richness coupled with sweet vanillan oak on the mid-palate. Most intriguing again is this long, crisp, almost drying finish. It is as if the wine causes you to suck in your cheeks. That's the wonderful natural acidity showing in the wine—very sexy to drink. The more I taste the wine the more it keeps developing, with flavors like sweet burnt lemon peel exploding in your mouth. I love this wine in a big Burgundy bowl that allows all these smells to pour forth. Obviously, I think the wine is lovely to drink now, but each month of bottle age seems to give it a new nuance. I think it will be lovely to come back to it in about three or four years and see how all those flavors have melded with each other.

1991 CHARDONNAY In many ways this is our 1990, except there is more—much more. The dream of all wine makers is to produce a wine with a personality all of it's own. Naturally the vineyard is the essential factor. This is truly Iron Horse Chardonnay. It has bouquet of brown cinnamon, allspice, pear, and passionfruit. It hasn't changed on the nose all that dramatically since last March when Joy and I seriously tasted the wines together for the book—only intensified. It is almost like lemon butter on the palate. Joy describes it as walk through the Casbah. I remain convinced that it will be a benchmark for us. A wine that can easily be kept for five to ten years and wish you had kept more.

1991 CUVÉE R This is the surprise of the vintage. Here is a wine that came out of nowhere to be the most interesting wine of the year. Cuvée R is a separate lot of Pinot Noir that we have been making since 1990. We began producing Brut Rosé in 1985, trying various techniques to create wine of vibrant color and unique bouquet characteristic. We tried making the wine with 100 percent Pinot Noir, leaving the juice in contact with the skins to give us the color and flavor we wanted. It was too fruity. We also tried adding bottled older Pinot Noir to a Brut Cuvée. It lacked vibrancy of color and flavor. We finally decided to make a special tank of Pinot Noir specifically for the purpose of making Brut Rosé. Raphael proposed using a technique called thermal maceration, which would provide a wine of deep color and berry flavor but with a minimal amount of astringency. The process involves crushing the Pinot Noir into an open top tank and heating the must to 38° C. This takes six hours of running increasingly warmer water around the outside jackets of the tank. When the must reaches the desired temperature, it is left to cool gradually overnight and is then inoculated with a special yeast and cool fermented. The result is an explosion of all kinds of berries—almost lollipop blackberry and strawberry combined. I was intrigued from the very beginning, but I had a lot of convincing to do to get Joy excited about labeling this small lot separately and selling it. However, everyone who tasted it loved it so much, she relented. The great story about this wine is that recently, when we sold the last few bottles at the retail room, one of the last customers proceeded to sell a few of his bottles of Cuvée R to another customer at a *profit*—right in front of Shirley. Now that is a hot wine. It is also a prototype of something I would like to continue to explore. This is a sophisticated Pinot Noir, but most of all a wine everyone is going to enjoy drinking.

1991 CABERNET I love cooking up a blend of all the different lots of Cabernet and Cabernet Franc for Joy. A bit of this and a bit of that and voilà! the 1991 Cabernet. Naturally it's only a snapshot. More than any other vintage that I have made, I find it has much similarity to a classic, young, well-made

Bordeaux. The aroma is Crème de Cassis. There is a smokiness perhaps stronger than normal because the samples are drawn off the top of the barrels. They always show more oak than in fact is distributed throughout the barrel. Although young, there is this creaminess that promises great depth of flavor. Because this is such a naturally balanced vintage, even with it's youthfulness it is beautifully proportioned. The Cabernet Sauvignon wines remind me of the 1982 vintage, which is only now beginning to show its full promise. The Cabernet Franc lots recall the 1987s, which were full and rich and have integrated beautifully with the Cabernet Sauvignon. If the 1991 can come close to the 1987 I will be a very happy winegrower.

—Forrest R. Tancer

ABOUT THE AUTHOR

JOY STERLING is the sales, marketing, and public relations director at Iron Horse Vineyards. She was raised in Paris by American parents, graduated from Yale, and had a ten-year journalism career before joining the family winery in 1985. She is married to Forrest Tancer, Iron Horse's wine maker, and they reside at the vineyard, located outside Sebastopol, in Sonoma County, California.